Dr. Masri is great at explaining and distilling the complicated science of climate change. He writes with personal conviction in a conversational style that is very accessible for general readers. Organized around answering climate change misconceptions, the book serves as a handy reference complete with footnotes to original sources. *Beyond Debate* is invaluable to climate advocates wishing to reach out to friends, neighbors and elected officials. The book not only increases readers' understanding, but provides hope by pointing to specific actions we can take both collectively and as individuals.

-Bob Taylor, Environmental Journalist

D0179299

In Praise of *Beyond Debate*

Written in an easily understandable and positive style, this concise and refreshing book explains what is true and not true about one of the most important environmental problems of our time, and offers approaches each of us can take to contribute to a more sustainable world.

-Dr. Arthur Winer, Distinguished Professor Emeritus
Environmental Health Sciences Department, UCLA School of
Public Health

After six years of steady climate advocacy, I thought I had heard it all, but *Beyond Debate* gives easy to understand explanations of things I've longed glossed over. It is a great read for people new to and not new to climate change science.

-Mark Tabbert, Citizens' Climate Education Governing
Board

Beyond Debate is a "must have" reference for environmental science educators and a great compliment for the classroom. More broadly, this book suits literally anyone seeking to have the necessary background to hold a well-informed conversation about climate change. Dr. Masri equips the reader with clearly presented science that has the power to put to rest, once and for all, commonly held misperceptions that continue to fuel public confusion and stall much needed climate solutions.

-Teri Osborne, Environmental Science Educator

BEYOND DEBATE

BEYOND DEBATE

ANSWERS TO

50 MISCONCEPTIONS ON CLIMATE CHANGE

SHAHIR MASRI

DOCKSIDE SAILING PRESS®

Newport Beach, California

DOCKSIDE SAILING PRESS®

Newport Beach, California

Newport Beach, California
www.docksidesailingpress.com
1A

Subjects: Climate Change, Global Warming,
Common Misconceptions

Cover photo: Hubbard Glacier, Alaska in 2012
Courtesy Dockside Sailing Press
Used with permission

In dedication to my mother,
who inspired in me a love for science and the environment,
and an unwavering passion to better the world.

Contents

Jobs & the Economy

Conflicting Evidence

Preface

Whether we believe the climate is changing, or that humans are the cause, we can all at least agree that climate is important—and critically so, allowing sun for our crops, rain for our streams, and so on. Because the climate is so important, almost everyone seems to have something to say about climate change, global warming, or whatever we want to call it—albeit *some* more than others! At times, such conversations can even get heated (no pun intended!). Isn't that weird? The climate can literally change the "climate" of a room, perhaps disrupting a family dinner or a picnic at the park. Uncle Bob say's the climate *always* changes. Aunt Jane points to government conspiracy. And your cousin calls them both crazy. Meanwhile, the children roll their eyes, turning instead to their iPhones.

In my career studying environmental science and public health, I've found it interesting to hear people's various perspectives on global warming and whether (or why) they believe the climate is changing. I've never been one to pursue arguments on the topic, but have instead found it more valuable to listen and hear why people feel the way they do. What kinds of factors or information cause people to think climate change is either a major threat or a total hoax? And of course, there are many people in between. As I write this preface, my local area is coming out of a record-breaking heatwave. Does this cause people to think of "climate change" or "human activity?" I'd like to know. I find these to be important questions to ask and conversations to have, which can help to positively move the dialogue forward.

While research takes most of my time, I'm a bit of a non-traditional scientist in that I've made it a point to not just study science, but to communicate that science to the public. All too often, scientists dedicate their careers to understanding and advancing an area of study, while their voices get channeled only through technical analyses and reports that the public never reads. How well the rest of the world comes to understand a given matter is therefore left at the mercy of journalists and the media to translate. This somewhat roundabout path from scientists to the media and then to the public is reminiscent of the game "telephone," in which a message gets whispered through a chain of people only to become distorted by the time it reaches the last person. I believe a similar dynamic has played out with climate change, albeit with added layers of complexity that we'll discuss in later pages. As a result, the climate conversation can at times resemble a jumbled mess, in which no one seems to get anywhere. It's no wonder people shy away from the discussion!

In this book, I've done my best to pool together 50 of the top misconceptions concerning climate change. The chosen topics reflect those that I've most frequently encountered in my personal conversations with people, online research, books, and polling of students and friends. I even went door-to-door to speak with neighbors! By assembling these claims and questions, and breaking them down one-by-one scientifically and in a simple, thorough, and compelling fashion, I hope to provide valuable insights about this incredibly important issue which has become *the* issue of our time. In addition to discussing the science and impacts of global warming, I've also highlighted a number of solutions that can help to curb greenhouse gas emissions and shift the world onto a more sustainable path.

While it may be best to read these pages in the order of their chapters, the book was designed so that this is not a necessity. I've done my best to let each chapter stand alone. Where prior chapters are helpful to understanding later chapters, I've been diligent to refer you to the exact chapter numbers where you can find supporting information. If, however, you're relatively unfamiliar with global warming or climate science, I recommend at least beginning with the introductory Climate Change 101 section. This will give you the foundation necessary to make the most out of the remaining chapters. Once you've got the basics, flip through the book in the order you prefer, letting your interest guide you!

Enjoy *Beyond Debate*. And importantly, share what you come to discover. It is only through sharing and conversing with our family, friends, and neighbors that we can expect to dispel the misconceptions around climate change and ultimately elevate the climate conversation.

Shahir Masri
Newport Beach, CA.

Climate Change 101

Although the climate is complex, scientists have come a long way in understanding its complexity. In fact, scientists have come to understand a variety of complex phenomena. It's thanks to scientists' sophisticated understanding of chemistry, physics, and engineering that we're able to pick up a phone to speak with someone halfway around the world, flip on the T.V. to watch our favorite athletes duke it out live, or take a nap in an airplane only to wake up in a foreign country. The world is complex, yet scientists have done an impressive job making sense of it. Understanding what influences the climate has been no exception. Let's take a moment to walk through the basics, discussing greenhouse gases, how they warm the planet, and the various factors that have led to this dilemma called global warming.

The Greenhouse Effect

If you've ever stepped into your car on a hot summer day to find the inside temperature about 20 degrees warmer, then you've experienced the greenhouse effect. Botanical greenhouses similarly stay warm even on the coolest of days, so long as the sun is shining—thus allowing us to grow tropical plants in climates that would otherwise be too cool. To understand how the greenhouse effect works, it's important to know that the sun emits "shortwave" radiation. This is a form of high-frequency light which packs enough energy to burn the skin, heat up the pavement, and allow plants to grow. It includes light within the so-called "visible" spectrum, which is the light our eyes detect in order to visualize objects. It's no coincidence we evolved to see within this range, since it is the most abundant type of sunlight on Earth's surface! As objects absorb high-frequency radiation, they become warm. For anyone who's ever basked in the sun, this is no surprise. What's important, however, is that when objects warm they too emit radiation, or light, even if the human eye can't see it. The light that warm objects emit is known as longwave radiation, or infrared light. Okay, well now that you've had your crash course in optics, let's get back to the greenhouse effect!

It turns out that shortwave radiation (sunlight) can pass uninterrupted through glass, while longwave radiation (from warm objects) cannot. The result is that sunlight passes into the greenhouse, warms the internal environment, but then is unable to escape. That is, after shortwave light passes through the glass and is absorbed by plants and other objects inside, which begin to warm, it gets released as longwave light. However, since longwave radiation can't escape back through the glass, it becomes trapped inside. Heat then accumulates and temperatures in the greenhouse go up!

In the case of Earth, our atmosphere is the glass. Well, not the whole atmosphere. Gases such as carbon dioxide (CO_2), methane, and nitrous oxide act as the glass of the

2

greenhouse. After sunlight penetrates through the atmosphere, warming the land and oceans, the heat gets redirected back out to space. Yet, as with the glass of the greenhouse, atmospheric gases prevent some of the outgoing light from escaping. The result? Temperatures on Earth go up. It's not surprising that such gases should earn the name "greenhouse gases." See Figure 1 for an illustration of this dynamic.

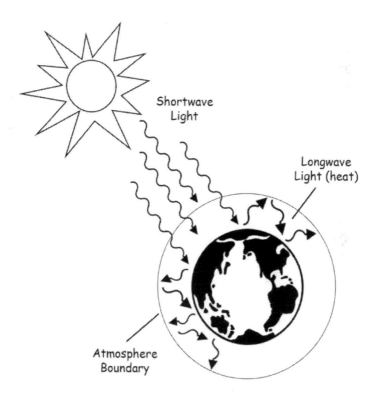

Figure 1. Schematic of the greenhouse effect. Shortwave radiation from the sun passes through the atmosphere. As Earth heats up, it emits longwave radiation that becomes trapped by greenhouse gases before it can escape back to space.

On Earth, our "glass" doesn't form a perfect heat barrier. The atmosphere is more like glass with windows in it. As we emit more CO_2 and other greenhouse gases, those windows begin to close, allowing temperatures to grow higher and higher. This is what's been happening for more than 200 years as societies have industrialized, human populations have grown, and farming and ranching have taken over. Each of these processes is associated with the release of massive amounts of greenhouse gases, as we'll discuss shortly.

The most important anthropogenic (human-caused) greenhouse gas in our atmosphere is carbon dioxide. It's most important not because its gaseous molecules are the most powerful heat-trappers—in fact, methane is 25 times more heat-trapping—but rather because it's the gas we emit the most of.[1] After taking into account the differences in their heat-trapping potential, carbon dioxide emissions from human activity account for 76% of total greenhouse gas emissions globally, compared to methane which only accounts for 16%.[2] Other greenhouses gases are even more heat-trapping. Nitrous oxide, for instance, traps heat about 300 times better than carbon dioxide, and chlorofluorocarbons (CFCs) are literally thousands of times more heat-trapping. But again, we don't release nearly as much of these gases as we do CO_2. In fact, combined, these gases account for less than 10% of our total greenhouse gases emissions. Water vapor is also a powerful greenhouse gas, and is in fact the most abundant greenhouse gas in the atmosphere. However, its role in global warming is limited for reasons we'll cover in Chapter 23. Thus, carbon dioxide has remained the primary target of attention as it relates to greenhouse gases and climate change.

The schematic in Figure 2 shows the dramatic rise in CO_2 levels that has occurred in recent decades—resulting in the gradual closing of our atmospheric "windows." Notice that CO_2 concentrations rise abruptly around the early 1800s— right alongside the industrial revolution. This is no coincidence, as we know that burning fossil fuels releases CO_2 into the air, and that society's use of fossil fuels ramped up dramatically around this period. Given what we know about greenhouse gases, we might expect this sharp rise in CO_2 to have led to an increase in global temperatures. Well, that's exactly what we've seen! It's not so complex or mysterious after all. The science is actually quite basic. So, why the "debate," you ask? Well, this is where climate change departs from the science and gets wrapped up in money and politics. But we'll discuss that later!

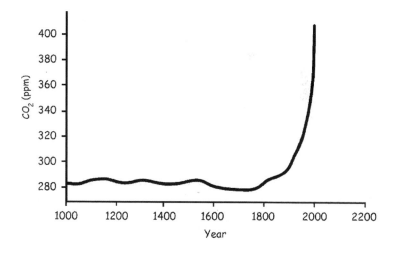

Figure 2. Schematic of carbon dioxide concentrations over the past 1,000 years.

I should mention that greenhouse gases are not inherently our enemy. Without their warming effects,

Earth's average temperature would be about 0°F (-18°C), or 60°F (15°C) lower than today—cold enough to turn the oceans to ice and render the planet inhospitable. It's only when we add *excess* greenhouse gas to the air that we destabilize the climate and run into trouble. In the case of carbon dioxide, *excess* arises when we tap into reservoirs of carbon-based oil, coal, and natural gas, reservoirs that have been locked beneath Earth's surface for millions of years.

To get an idea of what uber-high greenhouse gas levels on a planet look like, we can turn to Venus, which boasts a surface temperature of about 900⁰F (465 ⁰C)—hot enough to melt lead! Sure, Venus sits closer to the sun than Earth, but that only accounts for part of its higher temperature. The atmosphere on Venus is composed almost entirely of CO_2, making the planet especially efficient at trapping the sun's energy. The situation on Venus is that of a runaway greenhouse effect. As the hottest planet in our solar system, it's about as close to an apocalyptic underworld as you can get. Interestingly, the planet Mercury sits about twice as close to the sun as Venus, yet experiences cooler temperatures. How can this be? Mercury has no atmosphere. Thus, the greenhouse effect is missing and the planet can't retain any heat. It has the opposite problem of Venus!

Comparing planets is not only fun and interesting, it's also informative when it comes to understanding the importance of greenhouse gases and the climate. The conditions on Venus should give us pause and help us gain perspective on our own situation. Earth is by no means exempt from the fate of other planets—that is, to the fate of a runaway greenhouse effect. Former NASA scientist James Hansen talks about the prospect of Earth succumbing to so-called "Venus syndrome" in his book *Storms of My Grandchildren*.[3] It's a rather frightening discussion, but a worthy read!

Sources of Greenhouse Gas

Greenhouse gases arise from both natural and human sources. In the context of climate change however, it is not the natural sources that are of importance—except when discussing "feedbacks," which we'll get to shortly. Natural sources have always been around and have been relatively stable throughout human existence. It's with human activities of recent centuries, particularly after the industrial revolution, that we've begun to release exuberant quantities of carbon dioxide, methane, nitrous oxide and other gases into the atmosphere, thus upsetting the greenhouse balance. So, what activities are responsible for the release of these *excess* greenhouse gases?

Carbon dioxide is released every time we make a fire. That is, organic matter, whether it be firewood, plants, oil, coal, or natural gas, is made mostly of carbon. As these materials burn, their carbon content gets converted from solid carbon into carbon gas, or more technically "carbon dioxide" gas. Although we burn a lot of wood in the winter, this doesn't turn out to be the main source of human-related carbon emissions. Instead, fossil fuels take the cake—and by a long shot! Globally, burning fossil fuels accounts for about three quarters of carbon dioxide emissions. Most remaining emissions come from deforestation, since removing and burning forests releases carbon dioxide as well. We can break this down even further by sector. In the U.S., for instance, electricity production (burning coal and gas) and transportation (burning gasoline, diesel, etc.) each account for about a third of domestic CO_2 emissions, while the rest comes from industrial activities, home and residential heating, and other activities.[1] Let's turn to the next most important greenhouse gas—methane.

Methane is produced naturally from microorganisms that live in oxygen-deprived swamps and wetland soils. Unbeknownst to most people, human activities have created vast numbers of man-made swamps to grow rice. Yes, the kind of rice we eat! These crops grow in unique wetland-type environments, unlike most crops. These so-called "rice patties" turn out to be a source of methane comparable in amount to the emissions released by *natural* wetlands. Another major source of methane turns out to be cows, sheep, and other so-called "ruminants," which produce methane in their digestive tracts—the gas comes out of both ends! With over one billion head of cattle on Earth, these emissions add up.

Just as microorganisms produce methane in rice patties and in animals' digestive tracts, they also produce it when they decompose waste at the landfill. Because of the enormous amount of waste humans produce, on a pound-for-pound basis we turn out to be more efficient producers of methane than cows. Importantly, methane also seeps into the air when fossil fuels are mined and transported through piping systems. As of 2016, this was in fact the largest single contributor of human-related methane in the U.S., accounting for about 40% of emissions. Livestock comes in at around a quarter of emissions, with another third split about equally between landfills and other sources. Globally, over 70% of methane emissions come from human activities.

Nitrous oxide, another important greenhouse gas, is mostly produced from agriculture. That is, when farmers around the world apply fertilizers to the soil, some of the nitrogen compounds in the fertilizer get released as nitrous oxide into the air. As agriculture has become increasingly widespread with the sharp rise in human populations, atmospheric nitrous oxide levels have gone up and up. Nitrous oxide is also produced through high-temperature reactions, such as in internal combustion engines. In the U.S., agriculture accounts for about three-fourths of nitrous oxide emissions, followed by other sources. Globally, nearly half of nitrous oxide comes from human activities.

Of the most relevant greenhouse gases, CFCs are the only ones to have no natural sources in the environment. These chemicals are purely a product of manufacturing, historically used as refrigerants and inert gases for aerosol sprays, foaming agents, etc. Thanks to their role in degrading the protective ozone layer in the stratosphere (See Chapter 13), they've mostly been phased out of production. However, their replacement chemicals, HFCs, are also powerful greenhouse gases. Fortunately, they too are gradually being phased out. Nonetheless, these fluorinated gases remain in the atmosphere today, where they trap heat and cause warming.

The Rise of Greenhouse Gases

When we hear about CO_2 in the air, we often hear a unit known as "parts per million," or ppm. Though strange sounding, this just refers to the number of CO_2 molecules in the air compared to the number of air molecules. If the atmospheric CO_2 level is 200 ppm, for instance, it just means the air contains 200 parts CO_2 for every million parts air. Not too complicated after all! It sort of sounds like a baking recipe, right?—one part sugar, two parts milk, etc. Currently, atmospheric CO_2 levels are just over 400 ppm on average globally. That's only 0.04% of the atmosphere. Compared to the 21% oxygen in the air, that's just a drop in the bucket! So, who cares if we add a little extra CO_2 to the air?

To recap, greenhouse gases aren't new to the atmosphere, and their presence and heat-trapping abilities have in fact enabled nice, habitable temperatures here on Earth. However, throughout human history, carbon dioxide has made up only about 0.03% of the atmosphere. In the case of present-day global warming, what we're therefore talking about is a change in this very modest 0.03%. Over the last 200 years, the burning of fossil fuels has released enough CO_2 into the air to increase carbon dioxide levels to where they currently are—around 0.04%. While this is still a very small faction of the total atmosphere, it is not meaningless. Sure, greenhouse gases keep our planet cozy, but as we've all come to know in life, too much of a good thing can be bad. And that goes for greenhouse gases and the climate as well!

In discussing CO_2, it can be easy to dismiss the very low percentage or the units of "ppm" as insignificant. That is, what difference does it make if we add 10, 20 or even 100 ppm to the air? Or, who cares if atmospheric CO_2 goes from 0.03% to 0.04%? As it turns out historically, it can mean the difference between an ice age or no ice age. When discussing CO_2 and climate change, it's perhaps better to think about carbon dioxide levels in terms of percent changes, rather than differences in ppm or the absolute CO_2 amount. Understandably, most people simply can't relate with ppm and don't perceive low quantities as very important. But everyone understands percent changes.

For instance, since the 1800s CO_2 levels have increased by about 130 ppm, thanks mostly to the burning of fossil fuels. This somewhat abstract quantity fails to convey much meaning to the average person, and if anything sounds small and unimportant. But when we look at pre-industrial CO_2 compared to current CO_2 as a *percent change*, a different story emerges. The increase of 130 ppm turns out to be an enormous shift—a rise of 45%! This is a change we can all understand and recognize as significant.

If someone added 45% more salt to your dinner, you might love it or hate it, but you'd notice the difference. If you ate 45% more calories or exercised 45% more often, there's also little doubt you'd notice it. Change of course wouldn't be instantaneous, but rather take place over weeks or months. With Earth, a 45% increase in CO_2 is similarly a tremendous shift from the norm—a shift that we can expect to produce noticeable change. Except, rather than changing over weeks or months, we're talking years to decades. As the years pass, we're indeed observing such change. In fact, 17 of the 18 hottest years on record occurred in just the last two decades! How much temperatures and the climate will continue to change depends on how quickly we adopt renewable energy technologies (burn less fossil fuel), increase our energy efficiency, lessen our demand for resource-intensive food types, and in turn reduce our greenhouse gas emissions. But the sky is the limit—no pun intended!

In general, it doesn't take much greenhouse gas to

produce warming. Remember, an atmosphere with 0% compared to 0.03% CO_2 has been the difference between a frozen Earth and the comfortable planet on which human's adapted. Moving then from 0.03% to 0.04%, as we've done in recent years.... Well, you can only imagine the possibilities! And 0.04% isn't where it stops. Given the current rate of carbon emissions, this percentage will only continue to grow. The powerful influence of greenhouse gases on the climate, even at low concentrations, is somewhat akin to the influence of hormones on the body. Even the smallest differences in hormone levels can elicit dramatic changes in the body, affecting one's emotions, metabolism, and other processes.

Though we've focused on rising CO_2, the same global trends have been observed for other major greenhouse gases. Since pre-industrial days, the concentration of methane in the air has more than doubled due to human activities.[4] Similarly, while levels of nitrous oxides have rarely exceeded 280 ppb over the last 800,000 years, widespread agriculture has made concentrations grow sharply since the 1920s. Nitrous oxide levels today are about 330 ppb. The same can be said for CFCs and HFCs, which didn't exist at all before modern industrial activities. Greenhouse gases wouldn't be accumulating in our atmosphere, and therefore wouldn't be such a threat, were it not for their extremely long "atmospheric lifetimes." That is, many greenhouse gases such as carbon dioxide, nitrous oxide, and CFCs last a hundred or more years in the atmosphere before eventually degrading.[5] Methane, which lasts only about 10 years, is no better, since it just breaks down to form CO_2!

To contextualize our current predicament, we know that

greenhouse gases trap heat and warm the planet. And we know their concentrations have been rising dramatically since the industrial revolution. By increasing CO_2 and other greenhouse gases so sharply in recent centuries, we're in completely uncharted territory in terms of the climate—literally conducting a planetary experiment. How global temperatures will ultimately respond to such increases is any climate modelers best estimate. However, the estimates don't look pretty, and thus, a rapid reduction in emissions is needed. This will all become more apparent as you turn the pages of this book. But if you've made it this far, then congratulations—you already understand climate change better than most!

The Tipping Point

If you've heard of climate change, you've probably heard of the "tipping point." But what does this mean? To understand, you must first understand the concept of "feedback," and particularly Earth's "positive feedback" systems. You're all familiar with positive feedback whether you know it or not. Positive feedback is when a change in A leads to a change in B. That change in B then leads to a further change in A, which further changes B again. This goes back and forth as both A and B continuously reinforce each other—a sort of snowball effect. Besides snowballs, Earth has some positive feedback systems with tremendous implications to the climate. Let's take a look at a few and discuss how small initial changes can rapidly get out of control and send things down an undesirable path.

Snow Cover – As sun hits Earth, some of its light is absorbed and some is reflected. The pleasant climate we enjoy on Earth today is the result of a delicate balance between this incoming and outgoing energy. Snow and ice on Earth play an important role in this energy balance, serving as the "mirrors" that reflect much of the sun's energy. As greenhouse gas levels rise and cause warming however, these mirrors are melting and decreasing in size. As they melt, their reflective white surfaces are giving way and exposing underlying land and ocean surfaces, which absorb rather than reflect most light. This is where the dangerous positive feedback process kicks in. Replacing a reflective snowy surface with a heat-absorbing surface leads to more warming. With more warming, even more snow melts, leading to even less sunlight reflection and even more warming. The process goes on and on, the end result being higher and higher temperatures. It is a frightening path, but a path we're already initiating.

Water Vapor – The oceans have done us an enormous favor over the centuries by absorbing much of the carbon dioxide we've released into the air. As physics would have it, however warm water doesn't absorb as much gas as cold water. Therefore, as we warm the oceans, we reduce the ability of surface water to absorb and help offset atmospheric CO_2. On a global scale, warmer oceans absorbing less CO_2 has quite an impact, allowing for a quicker buildup of CO_2 in the atmosphere and even more rapid warming. The oceans play another important role. Warmer temperatures lead to the evaporation of more ocean water. Water vapor is a powerful greenhouse gas. So, as we warm the oceans, we increase the heat trapping capacity of the atmosphere, and in turn cause temperatures to rise even further. Another self-perpetuating feedback loop in motion!

Dying Forests – The rain forests represent an enormous source of stored carbon on Earth. As warming temperatures lead to the death of certain forests however, dead plant matter decomposes and releases this stored carbon into the air. Active deforestation is also contributing to this. Unfortunately, less forest means less carbon storage. This means more atmospheric carbon dioxide and higher temperatures. Higher temperatures can lead to even greater forest death, and so on. The cycle continues, again racing us to the precipice of a runaway effect.

Thawing Permafrost – This is potentially the most alarming feedback of them all. Within the soils of the frozen tundra is an enormous quantity of organic matter (partially decomposed plants and other organisms). While frozen, these organics pose no threat to our climate. Were the tundra to melt, however, decomposition would start, and this matter would release vast quantities of methane and carbon dioxide into the air. Recall that methane is even more heat-trapping than carbon dioxide. It's estimated that enough carbon is stored in permafrost to more than double the current level of carbon in the atmosphere.[6] Global warming has already caused permafrost in Alaska and elsewhere to begin thawing as many regions that were previously frozen year-round now experience above freezing temperatures. Carbon in the tundra represents a dangerously large source of heat-trapping gas that is best left in the ground.

This brings us to the so-called tipping point, or what is

often thought of as the point of no return. That is, the point beyond which humans will have any real control over continued global warming. Right now, the main driver of global warming is human activity. However, once we reach a certain point and unlock the carbon in the tundra, as well as propel many of these other positive feedback systems, humans will have little say in how much our climate continues to warm. Our efforts will be of negligible importance. Releases of permafrost methane, a shrinking of Earth's "mirrors," and a more humid atmosphere are just a few of the many processes that will secure the fate of our climate; that is, if we decide not to act.

Major positive feedback systems are already kicking into gear, the most visible of which is probably the rapidly disappearing sea ice of the Arctic. Again, however, triggering the melting of permafrost in the tundra may be the most frightening scenario, given the enormous reservoir of carbon waiting to enter the sky. Should we sufficiently set this ball in motion, a true tipping point will have been reached. We'll have unleashed a giant. Melting of glaciers would accelerate. Water vapor in the atmosphere would increase. And, of course, even more permafrost would thaw. These processes would only accelerate each other, as positive feedbacks do. It's an alarming prospect to say the least, but a very real one. And these are only *some* of the positive feedbacks that exist. All of this underscores the importance of current efforts to act on climate change— before it's no longer our decision.

While on the topic of climate feedbacks, it's important to mention that so-called "negative feedbacks" also exist, which have counteractive abilities that stabilize the climate. An example of a negative feedback is the increased plant productivity that comes with higher CO_2 levels, since plants "breathe" CO_2. As CO_2 increases, higher plant productivity helps to offset some of the rise. Another such feedback occurs when higher temperatures lead to more daytime cloud formation (due to more evaporation), and hence less sunlight reaching Earth. When the clouds hang around into the night, however, the effect goes the other way, since nighttime clouds tend to insulate Earth after sunset. All feedbacks considered, the negatives don't outweigh the positives, and Earth is warming at an accelerated rate. Scientists are not certain as to when the tipping point will have been reached. But it's probably best to not find out by stumbling upon it.

Natural Change

1

Greenhouse Gases Don't Really Trap Heat

This is perhaps the easiest myth to debunk because it requires a mere scientific experiment to disprove, and fortunately that experiment and many others have already been carried out. In fact, they were first carried out in the 1800s! But before we get to these experiments, let's provide a little context and history about the origins of climate science and how such experiments came to be.

Interestingly, research and understanding about global warming was born out of concern for potential global cooling. Nineteenth century European scientists observing glacial movements in the Alps noticed that in some areas glaciers appeared to have been much higher and widespread at one point. They wondered whether a prior ice age had occurred. And more importantly, might it return? An understanding as to what caused the climate to change over time was key to answering these questions.

Dating back even further, the earliest inkling of a

"greenhouse effect" came from a Genevan professor, mountain climber, and explorer named Horace Bénédict de Saussure. With a fascination for temperature and altitude, Saussure mused about why Earth's heat didn't all escape into space after sunset. To understand this, he constructed a "hot box," consisting of darkened cork on the sides and clear glass over the top. Resembling a modern-day greenhouse, the structure allowed light to pass in during the day, yet retained some of the heat at night. Perhaps, he wondered, the atmosphere behaved in the same fashion, allowing sunlight to pass through in the day, yet preventing the escape of heat at night. French mathematician Joseph Fourier also took to this idea. He admired Saussure's work and agreed with his hypothesis about the atmosphere. However, proving it mathematically turned out to be a difficult and frustrating feat, leaving Fourier to ultimately abandon the problem.

By 1837, the Swiss scientist Louis Agassiz declared that an ice age had indeed existed at one time, covering much of Europe with massive glaciers akin to those in Greenland. After relocating to the U.S. as a professor at Harvard, and demonstrating that past glaciers were responsible for carving the landscapes of the Great Lakes, Agassiz confirmed his declaration of a prior ice age, becoming arguably the founder of the notion of climate change.

The existence of a prior ice age and a possible "hot box" effect set the stage for what would soon become the first key experiments to demonstrate the warming effects of certain gases, or so-called greenhouse gases. At this point, we must turn to the work of a well-known Irish physicist named John Tyndall. Like his predecessors, Tyndall was obsessed by the movements of glaciers. He also wondered whether the atmosphere influenced temperatures on Earth. He got to work building an instrument called a spectrophotometer that would help him find answers. Consisting of a heat source, a receptor, and a small tubular chamber in the middle, Tyndall could test whether certain gases had the capacity to absorb infrared (longwave) light energy, and in turn trap heat.

The first gases Tyndall tested were those that are most abundant on Earth; namely, oxygen and nitrogen. After introducing each gas into the chamber, he found that neither gas dampened or absorbed the longwave light passing through. This was a disappointment as it didn't support the notion of a greenhouse effect. However, Tyndall pressed on. As luck would have it, light in those days (pre-electricity) was provided by burning coal gas, or "town gas." This was a mixture consisting mostly of methane. When Tyndall pumped coal gas into the testing chamber he discovered that the gas, though invisible to the eye, was not transparent to light energy. The receptor detected less energy when coal gas was present in the chamber, which meant the gas was trapping it. After testing water vapor and CO_2, he found the same result. These gases prevented some light energy from passing through. This was the proof Tyndall needed. Gases could in fact absorb longwave light, and thus trap heat. And there it happened in a lecture to the Royal Institution shortly after his discovery in 1859; Tyndall demonstrated for the first time in public an experimental account of the greenhouse effect!

Research by Tyndall and other scientists confirmed his earlier findings and built on the results. Not only could certain gases trap heat, they were also sufficiently abundant to have a major influence on Earth's temperature and climate. By the end of the century, the Swedish chemist, Svante Arrhenius, even calculated the global warming impacts that doubling atmospheric CO_2 levels would have on the planet. Without the benefit of a computer, his estimate of a 9-11°F (5-6°C) increase in global temperatures was surprisingly well within the estimates of modern science.

All of this, and we haven't even made our way to the 1900s! Although, I think by now you get the point. That is, the physics and light absorbing capacities of CO_2 and other greenhouse gases is no mystery and has been demonstrated repeatedly. It was proven and even publicly showcased over a century and a half ago. For those curious, you can conduct a similar experiment to that of Tyndall's in your own home. Simply get two thermometers, a couple of empty water bottles, and some CO_2 gas. When shining a proper lamp on the bottles containing either the air or CO_2, you'll find that after about a half hour the temperature in the CO_2-filled bottle is noticeably higher. It's not magic, it's the greenhouse effect! If you don't want the hassle of rigging your own experiment, check out one of the many fun video demonstrations online!

2

No One Really Knows What Prehistoric CO$_2$ and Temperature Were Like

Thanks to Charles David Keeling, we have reliable direct measurements of CO$_2$ dating back to 1957. As we'll discuss in Chapter 32, Keeling spent much of his career atop a Hawaiian volcano collecting such measurements. His famous "Keeling Curve" demonstrates that CO$_2$ has been increasing rapidly year after year. As for temperature, direct measurements from thermometers date back even further. In the U.S., for instance, the National Oceanic and Atmospheric Administration has been keeping temperature records for 138 years. This is great and all, but what about those graphs that show temperature and CO$_2$ levels dating back thousands and even millions of years? How can scientists possibly understand what the prehistoric atmosphere was like, and where does such data come from? It's actually quite fascinating! Let's have a look at a technique that uses ice cores.

In regions such as Greenland and the Antarctic, snowfall has been accumulating for thousands of years. When snow first falls, it is quite fluffy and full of air pockets. As the snow piles up, the pressure underneath increases, forming layers of compacted ice which, over time, essentially become time capsules of the past. That is, the deeper you go, the further into history you can see. Ice near the bottoms of major ice sheets represents snow that once fell hundreds of thousands, and even millions, of years ago.

If you're wondering how scientists access ice buried deep below the surface, it's simple. They drill vertically down using a large, hollowed out drill bit. Then, out come long segments of cylindrical ice cores. At a recent science exhibition, I got to hold a small fragment of an ice core that was 400,000 years old. Being the science nerd that I am, I politely asked the researcher to take our (the ice and my) photo! The oldest ice on record, however, has my chunk of ice beat by a long shot. It dates back some 2.7 million years and was excavated only very recently, in 2017, from a blue ice area in the Antarctic—beating the age of the previous record-holding ice core by a staggering 1.7 million years.[1]

Prehistoric ice is important for two reasons. First, it can tell us something about past carbon dioxide levels in the atmosphere, and second, it can tell us something about past temperatures on Earth. In terms of CO_2, the way scientists can discern what atmospheres of the past were like is through microscopic bubbles trapped in ancient ice cores. Though larger air pockets get driven away as fresh snow accumulates and compacts the underlying snow, microscopic air bubbles remain. At a certain depth beneath the surface, the ice becomes so compact that these bubbles essentially lose touch with the surface atmosphere, becoming trapped and isolated. In this way, ice core bubbles serve as little atmospheric samples from the past—nicely organized and preserved as if meant for the hands of science. To unlock the air inside the bubbles, researchers simply melt or crush the ice samples in the lab—each deeper layer representing an earlier and earlier point in the Earth's long climate history.

Ice core bubbles can tell us not just about past CO_2, but about all three of the long-lived greenhouse gases, including CO_2, methane, and nitrous oxide. When scientists compare the atmosphere of the most recent ice age with the post-ice age warmer period known as the Holocene (the current era), they find that the concentrations of all three gases were higher during the warm period. This fits in nicely with our understanding of the heat-trapping effects of greenhouse gases. Frighteningly, the levels of these gases have only continued to soar in recent times. In the case of CO_2 (Figure 2), a close look at ice core data spanning the last 800,000 years reveals that carbon dioxide fluctuated from a low of about 180 parts per million (ppm) to a high of 280 ppm at roughly regular 100,000-year cycles. At no time over the last 800,000 years did CO_2 exceed about 300 ppm—that is, until now.[2]

At the start of the industrial revolution just 200 years ago CO_2 levels were at 280 ppm, referred to as "pre-industrial" CO_2. This level means carbon dioxide was at one of its 100,000-year peaks. In the ensuing 200-year period, CO_2 did not hold steady or begin its expected decline towards 180 ppm. Instead, human activity took the peak even higher. Much higher. Because we've been burning fossil fuels and releasing billions of tons per year of carbon dioxide into the air, CO_2 levels now exceed 400 ppm. (See Figure 3).This is troubling because it means that in just 200 years we've raised CO_2 by an amount that usually takes thousands of years to occur. And we've done so at a point when we were already at a 100,000-year CO_2 peak. Carbon dioxide levels in the atmosphere are consequently over 25% higher today than they were at any prior 100,000-year maximum that Earth has seen for at least close to a million years.

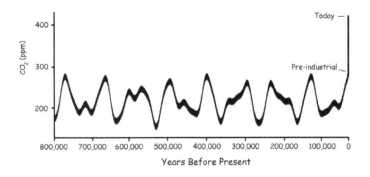

Figure 3. Schematic of carbon dioxide levels over the past 800,000 years, based on ice core date.

Now let's turn to temperature. Just as ice cores serve as time capsules through little bubbles of gas trapped deep beneath their surface, they also preserve information about past temperatures. In this case, it's the ratio of different isotopes of hydrogen in the water molecules that's important. What's an isotope? Let's pause for a quick science refresher!

If you've ever taken a chemistry course, recall that atoms are composed of a nucleus consisting of protons and neutrons surrounded by orbiting electrons. Elements are then named based on the number of protons in the nucleus.

28

Having said that, not all atoms of a given element are created equal. Some contain more or less neutrons than others. Atoms that have the same number of protons but different numbers of neutrons are referred to as isotopes. Different isotopes exist for all types of elements such as carbon, oxygen, hydrogen, and others. What happens to be important to our story are oxygen isotopes, since ice (frozen H_2O) is composed largely of oxygen. Now let's get back to ice cores and temperature!

The ratio of different oxygen isotopes in water happens to fluctuate with temperature. This is because so-called "light" oxygen tends to evaporate more readily and condense less readily than "heavy" oxygen. These different tendencies towards evaporation and condensation mean that the ratio of these isotopes in water and ice differs during periods of cooling versus warming. In polar ice cores, the math is quite simple—less heavy oxygen in ice means that temperatures were relatively cooler at the time that snow fell.

Similar inferences about temperature can be made about isotope ratios in the ocean. Because light oxygen evaporates more readily than its heavy counterpart, the seas become enriched in heavy oxygen as water continues to evaporate. Thus, high concentrations of heavy oxygen in the oceans tell scientists that light oxygen must have been trapped in ice sheets. The exact oxygen ratios can explain how much ice was covering Earth at different periods, indicating the timing of different ice ages. Of course, scientists can't teleport back in time to measure the oxygen in prior oceans. Therefore, to determine this they must measure the oxygen content of tiny oxygen-containing corals and shells deposited in layers of ocean sediments. Like ice sheets, ocean sediments are thick and abundant with information from the past. Just like ice cores, scientists drill "sediment cores."

Other so-called "proxy" measurements of temperature involve coral. Since the balance between strontium and calcium varies in coral according to temperature, scientists can measure the amounts of these chemicals in old coral and determine the ocean's past temperature. From ocean temperatures, scientists can understand what global atmospheric temperatures were like. Other climate related phenomena such as precipitation can be discerned based on the width, density, and isotopic composition of tree rings, while layers of ash and soot deposited in ice cores can tell scientists when gigantic volcanic eruptions and major forest fires occurred.

Using all of the techniques we've discussed, and still others we haven't covered, climatologists can confidently assemble a rather detailed painting of Earth's climatic history. To the assertion at the top of this chapter, I think we've sufficiently demonstrated that scientists can indeed understand Earth's prehistoric CO_2 and temperature levels. And it's by no means a guessing game. Rather, it involves highly advanced and sophisticated techniques requiring skilled scientists and specialized instruments. Technology and science at its best!

3

Volcanoes Are Warming Earth, NOT People!

I was actually at a chili cook-off when I first heard this assertion. I approached a registration booth for a (unnamed!) political party, figuring I would inquire about the then recent U.S. move to withdraw from the Paris Climate Accord. Upon inquiring, a kind middle-aged lady representing the party responded, "It's too expensive. The U.S. has already given a billion dollars to other countries. We can't afford to give more money for climate change." She proceeded to explain to me that volcanoes were responsible for warming the planet, not human emissions of greenhouse gases. We'll leave the "too expensive" part for a later discussion. For now, let's address this mix-up on volcanism.

The notion that volcanoes are heating the planet at least acknowledges what scientists have been saying for decades; namely, that the climate is warming. And it's true that volcanoes influence the climate. However, our friend at the chili cook-off had gotten the impact completely backwards. That is, volcanoes do not heat the planet, they actually cool it. This might sound counterintuitive. But consider that the burning of fossil fuels does not heat the planet by way of the hot flames involved in the burning process, but rather because the gas (CO_2) released from the burning process happens to trap solar radiation. Similarly, the flaming lava released from volcanoes has little impact on the climate. Instead, what matters are the gases released. And as it turns out, volcanoes emit sulfur dioxide into the atmosphere. This gas forms into products called sulfate aerosols, which reflect solar radiation (much like certain clouds) and in turn have a cooling effect on the climate.

Evidence of the cooling effect of volcanic eruptions can be observed in the recent temperature record. For instance, when Mount Pinatubo erupted in the Philippines in 1991, it became the second-largest terrestrial eruption of the 20th century and had a measurable short-term impact on the climate. That is, its release of over 20 million tons of sulfur dioxide created enough light-reflecting aerosol in the atmosphere to drop global average temperatures by nearly a degree Fahrenheit for the two years following the eruption.

In defense of our friend at the cook-off, there is something to the whole "volcanoes warm the Earth" notion. It turns out that in addition to releasing gases that cool the planet, volcanoes also release *some* heat trapping carbon dioxide, and volcanic eruptions have indeed played a warming role in Earth's geologic past. However, such influences have taken place over extremely long time scales (millions of years) and are essentially meaningless in the current context of present-day climate change. In other words, contemporary volcanic activity releases too little CO_2 to be of any concern. According the U.S. Geological Survey, present-day volcanoes release less than one percent of the CO_2 released currently by human activities.[3] That means that if you drew two volcanoes next to one another and scaled their sizes to reflect CO_2 released by present day volcanic activity and CO_2 released by human activity, they'd look something like Figure 4.

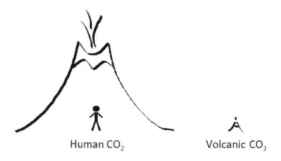

Human CO_2 Volcanic CO_2

Figure 4: Schematic of two volcanoes, with their area scaled to reflect CO_2 released by present-day human activity (left) and present-day volcanic activity (right).

The important takeaway here is that the sharp increase in temperatures observed over recent decades cannot possibly be explained by volcanoes. If anything, recent volcanoes have had a cooling effect. The "volcanoes" of most importance today are those that burn fossil fuels, destroy forests, and raise livestock—that is, humans!

4

Earth's Natural Cycles Explain Recent Warming

As we discussed in Climate Change 101, greenhouse gases are an important driver of climatic variation. But what about other influences? Earth's temperatures have gone up and down in the past. Is it possible that the current warming trend is just part of a natural cycle? Let's discuss.

Three distinct physical cycles have historically played a key role in Earth's major climate fluctuations. Collectively, these are known as the Milankovitch cycles, and include the following:

Precession – If you've ever spun a top on your desk, you'll notice as it slows it wobbles. Much like a top, Earth too spins with a slight wobble. Much slower than a top, of course! Earth completes one full wobble about every 26,000 years.

Axial Tilt – Earth is currently titled at about 23.5 degrees from vertical. This tilt is what gives rise to our seasons. As it turns out, this angle is not fixed, but fluctuates back and forth by a few degrees over time. One full fluctuation takes about 41,000 years.

Eccentricity – Thanks to the work of Copernicus in the 1500s, we all know that Earth orbits the sun. What is less known is that the shape of this orbit changes from oval to more circular at regular cycles. One cycle takes about 100,000 years to complete.

Notice the above cycles occur at frequencies of tens of thousands of years. Meanwhile, the Earth has warmed dramatically over the last two centuries. In other words, these three natural cycles have essentially remained unchanged over the recent warming period, and therefore cannot explain the recent warming trend. In fact, the current orientation of the Milankovitch cycles favors cooling rather than warming. But again, these cycles are gradual and play little role in temperature changes that occur over short time scales.

5

Solar Cycles Are To Blame!

You're now familiar with greenhouse gases and the Milankovitch cycles as being key influencers of the climate. But are there any other natural drivers of climate change? Yes, solar cycles! In contrast to the Milankovitch cycles, solar cycles occur at a much higher frequency—about every 11 years. In this case though, they occur too frequently to explain the gradual warming of the past couple of centuries.

Let's discuss another sun-related factor that has historically influenced the climate. That is, sunspots! Sunspots are dark colored disks that appear on the surface of the sun. When sunspots are more numerous, more energy is radiated from the sun to Earth, thus causing temperatures on Earth to rise. It's actually sunspot activity that is implicated as a likely cause of the recent Little Ice Age in Europe (See Chapter 41). Importantly, however, sunspot activity has not increased in recent decades. Therefore, sunspots fail to explain recent warming trends.

What then is the X factor driving current climate change? It can't be the Milankovitch cycles nor solar cycles as the timescales simply don't match up with present-day warming. And it can't be sunspots since sunspot activity hasn't suddenly increased. Let's turn to our earlier discussion and consider greenhouse gases, which are also known to be major drivers of climate variation. As it turns out, the level of greenhouse gases in the atmosphere correlates very well with the temperature changes we've observed. In a perfectly unbiased and politically neutral society, we would accept this with little resistance. It is quite clear and makes perfect scientific sense. In a world influenced heavily by major industrial players and political figures who have high stakes in the game, however, this sense has been muddied.

To sum things up for this chapter and the last, when we look at natural drivers of climate variation, they don't succeed in explaining the rapid increase in temperatures we've experienced in recent times. They occur either much too slowly (over tens of thousands of years), much too frequently (every decade), or are simply out of sync. What we are experiencing today is rapid and consistent warming on a timescale that correlates only with added greenhouse gas emissions.

Climate Conspiracy

6

Scientists Are "In" On A Climate Hoax!

This is an accusation that is admittedly rare to hear, and one that most would likely consider ridiculous. I was originally hesitant to even address it. But what the heck, let's humor it for a second and imagine the seamless logistics that would be required to pull off such a scam. Given the overwhelming volume of independent scientific studies published each year on climate change, a climate hoax would necessarily entail the collusion of literally thousands of scientists from various universities, governments, and other organizations over the entire world.

Scientists who are complete strangers to one another and would likely never meet would all have to be "in" on this secret and loyal to one another for some unknown cause. They would be agreeing to commit their lives and careers to an entirely made up pursuit, keeping their husbands, wives, children, students, friends, and others in the dark to prevent any "leaks" from happening. It's fair to assume that most scientists elected to spend a decade or more in college because they had an actual interest in their field and wanted to contribute to meaningful research. But this would all have to be cast aside. Quite a sacrifice, you say? Not until you consider that they'd also have to agree to very modest pay. The salaries of most scientists pale in comparison to other professions requiring similar or even less time in school, such as being a medical doctor, engineer, or lawyer. A pretty compelling deal, right? I think not!

Whether or not you could convince thousands of qualified experts to agree to these dismal conditions is one thing. Being able to pull it off is quite another. But we're having fun! So as farfetched as it is, let's pursue this a bit further and assume some entity managed to successfully get thousands of scientists onboard. This large global network would then need to communicate about their bogus research while avoiding any paper or internet trails, or leaks from some bozo telling his significant other. The U.S. Watergate scandal involved less than a hundred people, yet it leaked within months! The notion that thousands of scientists have managed to conceal a great climate hoax for decades is simply inconceivable.

Our discussion hasn't even addressed a possible motive. What could it be? Who would a climate hoax benefit? Given the obstacles and points already addressed, I'm not sure further discussion is worth our time. I'll leave the rest for others to ponder. I will just say that the winners certainly don't include the fossil fuel industry and other related sectors, which have more combined wealth than most entire nations. So whatever traction the "climate hoax" has gained has been at the expense of the most powerful industries in the world, and in spite of their best efforts to prevent it. Only one word again comes to mind. Inconceivable.

7

There's No 97% Climate Consensus

You've probably heard this percentage thrown around quite a bit to support the notion of a scientific consensus about climate change. While skeptics have repeatedly attacked this number, repeated survey data has consistently shown that approximately 97% of scientists indeed agree on the basics of climate science. Arguably the most comprehensive assessment to gauge scientific sentiment on climate change was carried out by The Consensus Project. This project was led by a University of Queensland scientist who analyzed over 12,000 peer-reviewed abstracts of climate change related studies published between 1991 and 2011.[1]

To digress briefly, an "abstract" is simply a brief summary of a scientific study. It typically appears as the first section of a science publication and runs no more than half a page. As for "peer-review," this refers to a rigorous process of scrutiny that a scientific study must go through before it can be published in the most respected scientific journals. For instance, if a geologist wishes to publish a study in a peer-reviewed geology journal, the journal editor must first pass the study to two or three fellow experts in that particular area of study to verify its merit. These so-called "reviewers" consist of rotating panels of voluntary scientists from other institutions who anonymously critique studies based on their methodological quality, relevance, among other factors. Getting a study accepted for publication by a peer-reviewed journal is a difficult and often drawn out process.

Now back to the Consensus Project. Abstracts from thousands of peer-reviewed studies were systematically compiled. That is, all abstracts in which the key phrases "global warming" or "global climate change" appeared were entered into the Consensus Project analysis. Each abstract was then reviewed by two independent international climate experts to identify whether the study either explicitly or implicitly rejected or supported the consensus view on climate change, or whether it expressed no opinion. The project also surveyed about 1,400 of the scientists who authored the various studies in order to obtain their perspectives on climate change.

As for the results, of the abstracts that expressed an explicit opinion on climate change, 97.1% supported the notion that humans are the cause of climate change. In terms of the author surveys, 97.2% shared the same view. It turns out the "97%" figure is quite robust. The Consensus Project indeed found a consensus, and overwhelmingly so.

In addition to the Consensus Project, a number of independent studies have reported similar findings, all in the high 90% range. Research tracking the consensus over time shows that this percentage has not remained constant.

In the early 1990s the consensus stood at around 90%. As of 2011 it rose to 98%. This suggests an evolution of opinion about human-caused climate change.

In addition to individual scientists, another way of gauging consensus is to look at leading scientific bodies. Those that agree with the consensus view on climate change happen to include the National Academy of Sciences (USA), National Center for Atmospheric Research (USA), American Astronomical Society, American Chemical Society, United Kingdom Royal Society, European Physical Society, U.S. Environmental Protection Agency, Science Council of Japan, Geological Society of Australia, American Association for the Advancement of Science, Academy of Sciences of South Africa, American Meteorological Society, American Geophysical Union, Académie des Sciences (France), Russian Academy of Sciences, Accademia dei Lincei (Italy), Chinese Academy of Sciences, Indian National Science Academy, Royal Society of Canada, and many more. As for science organizations with official positions refuting the consensus view, there were none that I could find. If the 97% consensus among individual scientists wasn't convincing enough, perhaps the 100% consensus among major international science organizations is.

8

Climate Change Is A Chinese Hoax!

If this phrase sounds familiar, it's because you've heard it echoed at the highest level of public office—yes, by President Donald Trump himself. While the office of the presidency naturally comes with credibility, there has been a more than palpable rejection by the current administration of climate science and the consensus that human activity is leading to warming. In terms of climate change, it's therefore important to apply a critical lens to the rhetoric that currently emanates from Washington.

Besides the President's own statements and decision to withdraw the U.S. from the Paris Climate Accord, evidence of his disregard for climate change can be seen by his initial cabinet appointments of former ExxonMobil CEO Rex Tillerson as Secretary of State and long-time Environmental Protection Agency (EPA) critic and fossil fuel industry ally Scott Pruitt to head EPA. Pruitt in particular has been very public in voicing his skepticism that carbon dioxide emissions are warming the planet. While serving as

Attorney General of Oklahoma, Pruitt in fact sued the EPA on 14 separate occasions, mostly over emissions regulations, and in several cases on policies designed to curb greenhouse gas emissions and slow climate change.

Now let's get back to the notion of a Chinese hoax. Besides pointing out the visible anti-climate science bias in Washington, what evidence is there to refute this claim? Quite frankly, too much to present in a single chapter. So I've instead chosen to lay out an illustrative timeline of U.S. and international concern over the climate. As you'll find, the history of awareness about the potential climate impacts caused by burning fossil fuels dates back quite far. Global warming is not so "new" after all. For a more thorough history of the science itself, return to the first chapter where we dive back even further to the 1800s.

It may come as a surprise, but as early as the mid-twentieth century, the science on climate change was sufficient to raise concern among scientists. By 1965, a report by the President's own Science Advisory Committee Panel on Environmental Pollution included a detailed discussion of fossil fuel combustion and rising CO_2 levels.[2] The report noted that "the present rate of carbon dioxide production from fossil fuel combustion is about a hundred times the average rate" and that "within a few short centuries, we are returning to the air a significant part of the carbon dioxide that was slowly extracted by plants and buried in the sediments during half a billion years [referring to coal and oil formed by ancient plant material]." According to the report, recent "atmospheric warming between 1885 and 1940 was a world-wide phenomenon." The document even highlights concern by some scientists of "catastrophic melting of the Antarctic ice cap, with an accompanying rise in sea level." Again, this was only 1965!

In 1972, the U.S. Atomic Energy Commission warned that rising CO_2 levels could "melt the polar ice caps" and "inundate the coastal regions."[3] By the end of the decade, the World Meteorological Organization convened what is now called the First World Climate Conference, or the 1979 World Climate Conference, which concluded that "it is now urgently necessary for the nations of the world to foresee and prevent potential man-made changes in climate that might be adverse to the well-being of humanity."[4]

In the U.S., June of 1986 (the month and year I was born!) marked an historic bipartisan hearing in which Republican Senator John Chafee opened by warning of "the buildup of greenhouse gases, which threaten to warm the earth to unprecedented levels. Such a warming," he went on, "could, within the next 50 to 75 years, produce enormous changes in a climate that has remained fairly stable for thousands of years."[5] The senator also stated, "There is a very real possibility that man—through ignorance or indifference, or both—is irreversibly altering the ability of our atmosphere to perform basic life support functions for the planet." Others who testified included the director of NASA's Goddard Center, Dr. James Hansen, as well as Dr. Michael Oppenheimer of Princeton; Dr. Robert Watson; and then-Senator Al Gore.

The 1960s, the 1970s, the 1980s—each clearly demonstrated our understanding of climate change and the impacts of burning fossil fuel. Since these early reports, conferences, studies, and hearings, the volume of climate science and calls for urgent action has only mounted. Consequently, the international community has become increasingly concerned about the climate, with many nations and states even taking independent actions to invest in alternative energies, regulate greenhouse gas emissions, and develop adaptation strategies to cope with sea level rise and other climate impacts. In short, global warming is not a Chinese hoax, or even a Chinese concern. It is an international concern, and one that dates back a half century or more.

9

Climategate – What About "The Emails?"

Those who witnessed the 2016 U.S. presidential election race probably want to hear no more about "the emails." In this case however, we're talking about a different set of emails—those concerning so-called "climategate." I was auditing a class at MIT when I first learned of this story. The professor explained that emails by climate scientists had gotten hacked, leading to a firestorm of controversy. He also mentioned that the story was overblown and misconstrued, noting that emails were being taken out of context so as to be used as ammunition by those determined to refute climate change. I would come to learn he was right. I shall explain.

It all began at the University of East Anglia, a public research university in Norwich, England, which houses the Climate Research Unit (CRU). The CRU was founded in the 1970s and is one of the world's leading institutions on the study of climate change. Consisting of a staff of around twenty research scientists and students, the Unit has produced a number of important data sets used by climate scientists, including the global temperature record, as well as developed climate models. One specific dataset is of particular interest to this story; namely, that of pre-1850 temperature data reconstructed using tree ring measurements.

In November of 2009, an unidentified hacker broke into the email server at the CRU, publicly releasing over a thousand email exchanges between scientists. The most incendiary of these emails was that by CRU scientist Phil Jones, which read.

"I've just completed Mike's Nature trick of adding in the real temps to each series for the last 20 years (ie from 1981 onwards) and from 1961 for Keith's to hide the decline."

At first glance, the email admittedly looks questionable. What "trick" is he talking about, and why would anyone "hide the decline?" Was Jones hiding the temperature decline in order to propagate a global warming conspiracy? Well this is the conclusion many climate skeptics immediately jumped to. However, if we're truly interested in answering this question, it's worth diving a bit deeper.

First, who is Mike and what's his "Nature trick?" Michael Mann, as he is more formally known, is a climate scientist and professor at Pennsylvania State University. In 1998, Mike published a study with colleagues showing temperature trends based on recent temperature and historic reconstructed temperature data. While recent temperature measurements are straightforward to obtain, thermometers only date back so far in time. Hence, reconstructing temperature trends using indirect measures—in this case tree rings—is a valuable tool for understanding trends over older time periods.

You might think it would be interesting to see historic and recent temperature trends plotted together in the same graph. Well, so did Mike! And this is just what he did. He combined both datasets into a single temperature graph, with appropriate labeling of course. The study was ultimately published in *Nature*—hence, Mike's "Nature trick." It was not a deceitful trick, but rather a trick of the trade, and a common one at that.

So what about this "hide the decline" phrase? What did Jones mean? Well, skeptics will tell you it is evidence that climate change is a hoax. Earth isn't warming. It may even be cooling. And Mike was trying to hide the temperature decline. However, you don't have to dig deep to discover that Mike wasn't even referring to temperature at all with that phrase. He was referring to tree ring measurements.

As a kid, you may have learned that by counting the rings in a tree stump you can determine the age of the fallen tree. This is because tree ring growth corresponds with the seasons. As it turns out, the density and width of these rings can also tell us a thing or two about past temperature. And when scientists analyze tree rings from around the world, a good indication of historic global temperature emerges. However, there is one exception. For a particular group of trees in the high northern latitudes, tree ring data began to depart from the norm. Around the 1960s, tree rings for this group of specimens no longer appeared to track local temperature. This so-called "divergence problem" has been widely discussed for years, potentially related to drought or air pollution that occurred during that period. However, the verdict is still out. It is this decline in tree growth that Mike was referring to. Not a decline in temperature.

Ok, fine, we're talking about tree rings. But still, why hide the decline? Was this scientific malfeasance? An independent review team funded by the University of East Anglia was established to find out. The team consisted of scientists without any affiliation with either the University or the Intergovernmental Panel on Climate Change. One scientist even included the head of research and technology at British Petroleum. The team ultimately found that they could replicate the CRUs findings using publicly available data, and that no bias was apparent by the CRU. An entirely separate investigation launched by Penn State, where Mike teaches, similarly found no evidence that Mike had ever falsified, or attempted to falsify, any data. The U.S. Environmental Protection Agency, U.K. House of Commons Science and Technology, National Science Foundation, and others similarly found no foul play.

The CRU data breach, according to the senior investigating officer of the crime, "was the result of a sophisticated and carefully orchestrated attack."[6] The hack was also quite timely. The theft occurred only weeks before the Copenhagen Summit on climate change. Because of such a coincidentally timed crime, many scientists, policy makers and public relations experts asserted that the release of emails was a smear campaign intended to undermine the climate conference. Or as Mike Mann puts it, climate change skeptics "don't have the science on their side anymore, so they've resorted to a smear campaign to distract the public from the reality of the problem and the need to confront it head-on in Copenhagen."[7]

10

"Glaciergate" Proves
A Climate Conspiracy!

It's quite commonplace for climate skeptics to either dismiss projections of future climate impacts or accuse scientists of exaggerating their claims. Some go as far as suggesting conspiracy. In most cases, such accusations are unfounded and misplaced. In the case of so-called "glaciergate," however, there is some merit to the claim. Although, not surprisingly, the circumstance was overblown. "Glaciergate" was merely an accident, rather than conspiracy. Let's look closer.

The story begins in Jawaharlal Nehru University, Delhi where an Indian glacier scientist gave an interview to *New Scientists* magazine. In the interview, Syed Hasnain asserted that all Himalayan glaciers might disappear by 2035 if the current rate of warming continues. As it turns out, this statement was incorrect. Though this slipup might seem insignificant, a cascade of unfortunate events laid the foundation for what would become full-blown "glaciergate."

The first event in this cascade was the publication of a 2005 World Wildlife Fund (WWF) report on Himalayan glacial retreat, which repeated Hasnain's statement, citing *New Scientist* as the information source. Had things ended there, we probably wouldn't be having this discussion. But that's not how the story unfolded. To the misfortune of everyone involved, this unsubstantiated claim found its way into the Fourth Assessment Report of the Intergovernmental Panel on Climate Change (IPCC), this time citing WWF as the information source. That's where our saga takes a sharp turn for the worse.

IPPC reports are held under high esteem for their rigorous scientific nature and scrutiny. The reports are meant to source mostly from peer-reviewed scientific studies and have a system in place for ensuring this. However, in this case, a false claim from a non-peer-reviewed source slipped passed the IPCC radar. For context, we're talking about only a single statement in a 3,000 page report. But it was an error nonetheless, which did not belong in the report.

It probably goes without saying that this mishap didn't go unnoticed. Instead, it made headlines, fueling the fire for those who allege "climate conspiracy." The unfortunate side story to the exaggerated claim about retreating Himalayan glaciers is that the region *is* in fact experiencing accelerated melting. While the Himalayan glaciers are not expected to disappear by 2035, they're nonetheless shrinking more and more rapidly. This reality should not be overlooked, especially considering that these glaciers are the source of drinking water, irrigation and hydroelectric power for some

1.5 billion people, or nearly 20% of the world's population.[8] In the case of "glaciergate," this part of the saga was missed.

11

The IPCC Is Corrupt And Misleading!

As already mentioned, the Intergovernmental Panel on Climate Change (IPCC) is a highly respected international body to which thousands of scientists from around the world contribute. IPPC reports are therefore regarded as highly credible and essential to understanding the various aspects of climate change. Nonetheless, and perhaps not surprisingly, there are some who accuse the IPCC of being either fraudulent or exaggerated. Rather than "agree to disagree," let's grab our magnifying glass and see how these accusations stand up to fact.

In terms of exaggeration, a comparison of IPCC projections with reality will show that in most cases IPCC projections are very accurate and, if anything, err on the side of being too conservative. This is the case for important projections about the rate of sea level rise, carbon dioxide emissions, and melting of Arctic sea ice. What we're seeing is an increased rate of these phenomena, which does not support the notion that IPCC reports are exaggerated. To site one example, a 2012 study comparing IPCC projections of sea level rise with actual observations over the 1993-2011 period showed the rate of actual sea level rise to be over 60% higher than that predicted by IPCC.[9]

Other attacks on IPCC relate to its general credibility. We discussed the case of the Indian scientist whose false statement made its way into an IPCC report. In this instance the IPCC was in error, and many criticisms were deserved, albeit talk of conspiracy was still unfounded. In other instances, accusations were outright false. In *How to Change Minds About Our Changing Climate*, authors Seth Darling and Douglas Sisterson highlight a number of examples that are worth repeating.[10]

The first false accusation involves the Fourth Assessment Report in which IPPC states that "up to 40% of the Amazonian forests could react drastically to even a slight reduction in precipitation." The reference for this statement happened to be another WWF report. Given the previous mishaps with WWF discussed in Chapter 10, this was fodder for vicious attacks by some groups, accusing IPCC for once again citing an "unscientific" source. However, in this case the WWF report was not based on a loose statement. Rather, WWF cited a 1999 peer-reviewed report published in *Nature*, which was consistent with other publications. In this case, accusations against IPCC were entirely unfounded.

Another example has to do with the so-called Medieval Warming Period, which is a block of time spanning about 950 to 1250 A.D. During this time, global average temperatures were relatively warm. In an early IPCC report, this period was depicted in the form of a rough illustration of temperature over the last 1000 years. By rough I mean that it was not a plot of actual temperature data. Rather, it was a schematic that didn't even contain a numerical axis. In the schematic, it appeared that the Medieval Warming Period was warmer than present-day temperatures.

In the next IPCC report, the schematic was gone; replaced instead with a diagram of actual temperature measurements. This is a good thing since we'd rather see data-based graphics rather than rough sketches. However, some were not so happy. In the original depiction, temperature during the Medieval Warming Period appeared slightly warmer than today. According to the new plot of actual data however, the period was indeed warm, but not as warm as today's temperatures. Critics accused IPCC of hiding the real data. But far from "hiding" the data, they were improving their depiction of it.

The original schematic was taken from a 1982 book called *Climate, History, and the Modern World*, by H.H. Lamb. Two facts about the original schematic are important to note. First, Lamb's temperature plot only considered average temperature leading up to 1950. That is, the graph didn't include modern temperatures, which is the period during which we've seen the greatest increase in greenhouse gas emissions and temperature. The graph therefore left out most of the "warming" part of global warming. Second, the graph was based on temperatures in England, not the entire globe. We should be pleased that IPCC replaced this outdated regional depiction with something more scientific and globally relevant. If you want to learn more about the Medieval Warming Period, turn to Chapter 40!

Doubt

12

Climate Change Is Just A "Theory"

This comment underscores an important distinction between the way that the public and scientific community use the word "theory." In the language of the everyday non-science person, a theory is basically a hypothesis or idea. "I have a theory as to why my dog always barks at the fence!" or "Jane's theory on weight loss doesn't seem to be working." Such uses of the word are all fine and dandy, but when you ask a scientist about its meaning, you'll find it has a strict definition and is used much more sparingly.

In science, a theory is much higher on the totem pole of ideas than a hypothesis. A theory is a hypothesis that has been tested and retested using the scientific method. Only after a hypothesis has stood the test of time and rigorous scrutiny, and gained widespread acceptance in the scientific community, will a hypothesis transcend into *theory*. So when scientists speak of the theory of climate change, they are not speaking of a whimsical idea held by a few. Rather, they are speaking of a well-grounded hypothesis that has been rigorously and repeatedly studied and ultimately gained acceptance among the community of climatologists, oceanographers, glaciologists, and the like.

Oversight of these different interpretations of *theory* has had unfortunate consequences when scientists get interviewed about climate change by the media. Talking about climate change as a *theory* is a perfectly natural and accurate use of scientific language according to the climatologist. Unbeknownst to the scientist, however, the public may hear *theory* and infer that climate change is still speculative—a mere idea or hypothesis. This situation can happen all too often and ends up fueling climate denial. If only we could get a translator in the room!

13

The Atmosphere Is HUGE, We Can't Possibly Affect It!

While the atmosphere seems infinite, consider this. On a planet that spans 25,000 miles around, the bulk of our atmosphere (99%) is only 18 miles high. That's the length of just 300 football fields! While our eyes can see as far as the nighttime stars, our own atmosphere is nothing more than a thin veneer around the planet. Having said that, the above claim can easily be debunked in a number of ways. We can take a quantitative approach and compare the mass of the troposphere to total pollution emissions and see that humans have indeed released enough CO_2 to alter the atmosphere. Or, we can skip the boring stuff and simply look at recent history, which proves the same case. Take the hole in the ozone layer for instance. For those old enough to remember, you'll recall being told that hairspray cans were bad for the environment. What was that all about? You may also remember hearing about acid rain. Let's discuss these stories to better understand the ability of humans to alter the sky.

The Ozone Story

In the 1920s, General Motors scientist Thomas Midgley Jr. engineered a safer chemical alternative to replace the toxic and flammable ammonia, chloromethane, and propane substances used in refrigeration processes. Teaming up with DuPont, production of the newly engineered "chlorofluorocarbons," or CFCs, began quickly. Flying under the trade name Freon™, CFCs became the preferred ingredient in home and car air conditioners, and by post-WWII were being used as propellants for spray paints, bug sprays, hair sprays, foaming agents, and other products. Heralded for their non-reactivity and low toxicity, CFCs were ideal for any products and processes requiring pressurized gas. And by the 1970s, CFC production reached one million tons worldwide.[1] Fortunately, as industry ramped up CFC production, a group of curious scientists at the University of California, Irvine (my current place of employment!) asked an important research question. Where were all these CFCs winding up?

Professor Sherwood Rowland, with his postdoctoral research fellow Mario Molina, instantly went to work on this conundrum and, before long, found that CFCs, when released, would ultimately travel to the upper atmosphere and wreak havoc on the protective ozone layer.[1] Their work was confirmed in 1985, when a separate team of British scientists discovered the great "ozone hole" over the Antarctic. CFCs, given their non-reactive nature, had been accumulating in the atmosphere over time, drifting higher and higher until ultimately escaping the atmosphere as we know it. That is, they made their way above the troposphere, which is where animals live, winds blow, and planes fly, into a region of the high, relatively stable sky known as the stratosphere. It is here that CFCs would meet their end and where Rowland and Molina warned of catastrophe.

The stratosphere houses the ozone layer, an incredibly important gaseous layer that absorbs harmful high-energy sunlight, thus protecting us Earthlings. It was in fact the formation of the protective ozone layer some 600 million years ago that enabled the gradual evolution of land animals from their former oceanic dwellings. However, with the creation of CFCs this incredibly important region of the atmosphere would come under grave threat. While CFCs are non-reactive at ground level, the stratosphere with its high-intensity sunlight truly brings these chemicals to life, and not in a good way!

When CFCs are subjected to high-energy sunlight, they split apart, sending their chlorine atoms off to wonder alone in the atmosphere. Kind of sad, right? Well these atoms don't stay loners for long. They quickly interact with and destroy our beloved ozone molecules. Frighteningly, a single CFC molecule is capable of destroying 100,000 ozone molecules! This is a very bad thing if we care about our protective ozone layer. Low and behold, with increased research and understanding of this photochemical process came the discovery of the notorious ozone hole, ultimately earning Rowland and Molina the 1995 Nobel Prize in Chemistry.

The ozone hole is not really a hole per se, but rather a massive area of depleted ozone. Due to Earth's climate and wind patterns, this hole fortunately exists mostly above the poles where relatively few people live. The greatest depletion by far exists over Antarctica, extending into southern New Zealand and Australia. In such regions, it is increasingly important to wear extra sunscreen to protect against harsh sunburns and skin cancer.

Fortunately, the discovery of the ozone hole led to immediate concern and action internationally. In 1987, following a global summit, the Montreal Protocol was born, and 57 countries agreed to cut CFC production by half. In the years to follow, even tighter and more widespread restrictions came into place, ensuring an even quicker phase-out of these destructive gases. While some initially speculated as to the disruption a CFC ban would cause to industry and the economy, it was not long into our understanding of CFC's harmful effects before DuPont engineered an ozone safe substitute for the chemicals.

By the early 1990s, CFC production had dropped precipitously, as intended. But because CFCs can last 50 to 100 years in the atmosphere, they are still abundant and wreaking havoc in the sky to this day. As of this writing, a large ozone hole still exists. Fortunately, however, ozone destruction has declined, and the ozone layer is expected to return to its 1980s levels by the end of the century.[2]

All told, we had a major problem, but quickly recognized it. It took less than 15 years from the time that basic scientific research uncovered the ozone problem (1973) to the time that the international community responded with a treaty (1987) and a plan to fix it. We listened to our scientists and took action, leading to a rapid decline of CFC use. The ozone hole is now healing, and life on land can resume. This is unquestionably a success story!

What were the lessons learned? Well first of all, human

activity is indeed capable of altering the atmosphere in critical ways. And recall, annual emissions of CFCs totaled to just one million tons per year during the peak of CFC use. In the case of climate change, annual carbon dioxide emissions from burning fossil fuels alone exceeds 30 billion metric tons—and that's not considering other emissions sources and greenhouse gases. Such pollution is more than enough to alter the atmosphere and has already done so in meaningful ways. Other lessons from the ozone experience are that widespread international cooperation can solve even the most dire environmental crises. In the case of ozone, however, nations were wise in listening to the collective message of the scientific community. The message was not convenient, but nations heeded it nonetheless. And in the end, industry continued to prosper. Banning CFCs did not cripple the economy, but rather spurred technological innovation while reducing pollution. It was a victory all around!

The Story of Acid Rain

Another example of humans harmfully altering the atmosphere through industrial pollution has to do with sulfur emissions and acid rain. This story again bears close resemblance to the situation we face today with carbon emissions and climate change. The sources of sulfur emissions are even the same as those that emit CO_2, namely, the burning of fossil fuels.

While the story of acid rain has a long history dating back to London in the 1850s, it did not begin to gain widespread attention in the U.S. until the 1970s, after decades of industrial expansion and economic growth led to increased electricity demand and, in turn, more fossil fuel combustion (electricity is mostly produced by burning fossil fuels). It goes without saying that fossil fuels are not clean. Given their long stint underground (millions of years), they tend to be far more than pure hydrocarbons. Mercury, sulfur, vanadium, and nickel are just a few of the impurities found in fossil fuels. Most important to our story, however, is sulfur.

Sulfur occurs naturally in the ground and hence makes its way into fossil fuels. Coal in particular contains high levels of sulfur. When burned, sulfur is released into the atmosphere in the form of SO_2. Historically, coal-burning power plants have been the leading emitters of SO_2 to the air. Who cares if SO_2 is in the air? Well, besides being toxic to inhale, the chemical mixes with water vapor in the air. This is where the "acid" part of the story comes in. SO_2 plus water makes sulfuric acid. Clouds that form in areas contaminated with heavy amounts SO_2 therefore become acidic. When these clouds precipitate—you guessed it— acid rain!

Because of the rampant use of coal in the U.S. and Europe, acid rain became an enormous problem in many countries. Such rain wreaks havoc by ruining soils, damaging plants, and acidifying lakes and streams (in turn killing fish), which has damaging ripple effects across entire ecosystems. Germany is an infamous example of ecological catastrophe, where heavy sulfur pollution and smog resulted in the near decimation of its magnificent Black Forest. The destruction was known as "Waldsterben," or "forest death," by locals. Acid rain also damages property. This was a particular issue in Europe where famous historical statues and monuments were literally dissolved by acid rain originating from nearby industry.

In North America the story is similar. Heavy coal use for energy production transformed our skies. And because air pollution doesn't abide by political boundaries, much of our acid rain problem became Canada's problem too. By the late 1990s, acid rain had led to the acidification of an estimated 14,000 lakes in Canada and thousands more in the U.S. In the New Jersey Pine Barrens area, more than 90% of streams were acidic, while up to 20% of lakes in New York's Adirondack Mountains were deemed "unsuitable for the survival of sensitive fish species."[3]

The so-called transboundary pollution problem between the U.S. and Canada ultimately led to the bilateral Canada-United States Air Quality Agreement of 1991 in which each country pledged to major emissions reductions. The Clean Air Act Amendments of 1990 similarly targeted SO_2 with the implementation of a cap-and-trade system requiring companies to clean up their acts. Thanks to recognition of the pollution problem and subsequent action, SO_2 levels have been dropping for decades. Consequently, acid rain has dissipated considerably, with many ecological areas no longer under threat. Compared to 1980, today's average SO_2 levels in the U.S. are lower by almost 90%. Nitrogen oxides, the other major acid rain precursor (also from burning fossil fuels), has seen 60% reductions thanks to similar efforts and regulations.

This story is useful to recall because it again reminds us that the atmosphere is not limitless in its ability to absorb waste. While visibly infinite, all of its wonder—the wind, the rain, the clouds—exists within a thin layer just miles from Earth's surface. Similarly, the pollution we emit stays in this thin layer. It does not drift into outer space, or even to the upper reaches of the blue sky, as we might imagine. In short, humans *can* influence the makeup of our atmosphere. We have in the past, and we are currently.

The ozone and sulfur stories are also noteworthy because they suggest a fairly good track record by our atmospheric scientists. Our scientists have gotten it right and rescued us from disaster more than once in the past. This same group of scientists, joined by many others, is now saying we've got a major climate problem on our hands caused by greenhouse gas emissions. Perhaps it's worth listening!

There is one key difference between the acid rain problem of the past, and the climate problem of the present. And unfortunately, it doesn't play to our advantage. When SO_2 is emitted to the atmosphere, it lasts only a matter of days before dissipating. CO_2 on the other hand lasts over a hundred years. The implications of this are enormously important. In the case of sulfur, it means that if we decide to halt emissions today, we can expect to reduce acid rain by the end of next week. For CO_2, the same cannot be said.

Because of its longer lifetime as well as the dynamic relationship between CO_2 in the air and ocean, not to mention positive feedback effects (See Climate Change 101), a decision to halt our carbon emissions today would not result in any meaningful reduction in atmospheric CO_2 and the greenhouse effect for decades if not centuries to come. And a complete reversion to pre-industrial temperatures and CO_2 would likely take thousands of years. By this time, who's to say what'll have happened to the remaining glaciers, sea level, and global temperatures? Like diamonds, CO_2 emissions are forever! It's why the decisions we make today about global warming are of such critical importance.

14

The Scientists Have Got It Wrong!

Although scientists in my experience tend to be the fastidious "triple-check everything" type of people, I will concede that scientists nonetheless make mistakes. However, in light of individual scientists perhaps erring here or there, it would be highly unlikely for an entire community of scientists to all err in the same direction. It's even less likely that a large international body composed of thousands of scientists would miss the mark. In the case of climate change, the Intergovernmental Panel on Climate Change (IPCC) draws on the work of literally thousands of scientists investigating various aspects of the climate problem, from oceanography, glaciology, and physics to atmospheric chemistry, ecology, and numerous other disciplines. With this level of collective expertise, it is all the more unlikely that we'd get an erroneous message from the science. The climate issue is actually a rare case in that we have an organization such as the IPCC that is dedicated entirely to reviewing and reporting on the state of climate science every few years. This added step of review and assimilation of the science serves to ensure confidence in interpreting what scientists are finding, and weighing the evidence accordingly.

It's also important to remember, as was just discussed in the prior chapter on ozone and sulfur emissions, that our earth and atmospheric scientists have a remarkable track record. They've gotten it right several times in the past, helping us to avert ecological catastrophe. This ought to give us more, *not* less, confidence in their judgement of climate change and the impacts of greenhouse gas emissions.

15

There Is Still "Uncertainty" About Climate Change

While it's true that scientists often discuss "uncertainty" when covering climate science, this word, like the word "theory" discussed previously, is fraught with misunderstanding. In science, the word has a technical meaning born from statistical analysis that is quite different than its use in everyday language. It's another case where we need a translator in the room!

In science, uncertainty, sometimes called percent uncertainty, is taken as a measure of what is called statistical significance. If results of a study are not statistically significant, it means they may have occurred by mere chance, called chance findings. In this case, good luck getting your study published! To know whether results occurred by chance, uncertainty is usually accompanied by a percentage—typically 5%, but sometimes 10%. These percentages are customary cutoffs that scientists use to decide whether results can be trusted or not. Although, scientists do not "trust," they merely have varying degrees of "confidence." Confidence, like uncertainty, has a technical meaning in science. The two correspond oppositely with one another. Instead of describing 5% uncertainty, one could express 95% confidence.

I won't bore you with how percent uncertainty and confidence are calculated. Suffice it to say they depend on the number of measurements collected and the degree to which those measurements differ from a separate set of measurements, usually some overall average or data from a control group. For instance, our confidence that this year's average temperature was "significantly" higher than last year's average depends how different the two averages are from one another and how many measurements were used to calculate the two averages. After carrying out calculations using this information, scientists can identify uncertainty levels and establish confidence about their results.

A 95% confidence level is a rather conservative percentage. For instance, 85% scientific confidence is probably sufficient to convince most people of something—say, an association between inhaling some chemical and developing cancer. But for scientists, it's not enough. Hence, 90-95% confidence is the rule of thumb.

Having 95% confidence is very powerful. As I mentioned, most would be fine with lower confidence. If the fire department told you they had a 50% confidence that your house would burn down in your lifetime—perhaps due to a highly flammable construction material—you'd probably call your local real estate agent and vacate in the near future. Similarly, you'd probably change your diet if doctors were 75% confident it would lead to midlife bladder cancer.

It's unlikely that you'd fixate on the "uncertainty," even though in these examples they're relatively large (25-50%). Yet, for some reason with global warming, climate skeptics often cite small 5-10% uncertainties as reasons for inaction and "business as usual."

In many cases, the public is innocently unaware of the specifics behind the term "uncertainty" as used by scientists. In everyday language, uncertainty means "unknown," "unsure," or "inexact". Most aren't familiar with the different confidence levels and 5-10% cutoffs that scientists apply. Similarly, when scientists discuss uncertainties in their research, they often forget that their audiences may include non-scientists who are unfamiliar with scientific uncertainty, and who instead interpret the scientists as being unsure of their work. Who cares about the science if researchers aren't even sure of what they're finding? Hence, a major disconnect!

In addition to confusion over the meanings of uncertainty and confidence, there is often a misunderstanding as to what exactly scientists are uncertain or confident about. For instance, people who hear about uncertainties of climate change naturally assume there is uncertainty about the fundamentals of climate science. In some cases, the media is to blame. Nonetheless, it's an erroneous interpretation that needs correcting. The science is very sound and consistent on the fundamentals of climate science. We know that greenhouse gases trap heat, and that greenhouse gas levels have been rapidly going up for over two centuries due to human activity. We know that glaciers are melting, and that sea levels are rising as a result. Where the uncertainty lies is around how rapidly these trends will progress. We discussed how uncertainty and confidence have statistical meanings, but scientists also use the terms to describe the range of estimates generated by different forecasting models. Let's take a look at an example from a recent climate report.

In its Fourth National Climate Assessment, the U.S. Global Change Research Program noted that "no single physical model is capable of accurately representing all of the major processes contributing to GMSL [global mean sea level rise]."[4] For this reason, the so-called U.S. Interagency Sea Level Rise Task Force estimates future sea level rise based on six possible scenarios. The best-case scenario predicts about one foot of sea level rise by 2100. This scenario assumes that sea level rise will continue at its present rate of about 0.12 inches/year (3 mm/year). The other five modeling scenarios assume sea level rise will increase to somewhere between 1.6 and 8.2 feet (50 and 250 cm) by 2100. These scenarios assume the rate of ocean rise will not remain flat (same as today's rate), but will instead pick up in the coming decades to around 0.2-1.7 inches/year.

Based on the range of these projections, a scientist might assign "high confidence" to the conclusion that sea levels will rise by 1.6 to 8.2 feet by 2100, because five of the six models forecasted within this range. By the way, these latter forecasting scenarios are the most likely if recent history is any indication. The last few decades have not shown a stable (or flat) rate of sea level rise. The rate has increased as the rate of glacial melt has increased. Nonetheless, this example reflects another use of the term *confidence*. One could also speak of *uncertainty*, since the models each produced different estimates. This would be a common use of the word as referenced by climate scientists, and scientifically it doesn't detract from the overall message. You'll notice *none* of the models predicted zero sea level rise or lower sea levels. This is because, despite some uncertainty, evidence points to RISING seas.

Other uncertainties exist about how much the globe will warm over the coming decades. Will it warm by two degrees or four degrees? Similarly, it's not certain as to how much of the Greenland or Antarctic ice sheets will disappear by the end of the century. But we know it won't be zero, and most likely will be substantial. And of course, these are key factors influencing sea level rise. However, not knowing how fast these factors will accelerate is not the same as not knowing whether they are occurring or will continue to occur. This is an important distinction. Climate change is indeed occurring, and human activity is indeed the primary cause. Questions of uncertainty are thus rooted in the extent of impacts and damages we can expect moving forward.

It's also worth noting that in science, 100% certainty is virtually impossible. Even when statistical uncertainty is close to zero, most scientists will not tell you that something is "certain." It's even rare to hear a scientist tell you something "causes" something else, because the word "cause" suggests absolute certainty, which science cannot demonstrate. Even when 99% confidence exists, scientists are reluctant to say X *causes* Y. This is because science looks at statistical associations and relationships between variables—the "likelihood" that changes in X will produce changes in Y. Rather than X *causing* Y, scientists are trained to say X is *associated* with Y. This reluctance to speak of "causes" again has the unfortunate drawback of conveying to the public a sense of being "unsure" about the data. In actuality, the reluctance is a mere technical nuance that stems from scientific training. It's just scientists being scientists.

If you've ever watched a televised climate debate, you'll notice that "scientists being scientists" can have detrimental effects when it comes to convincing the public about global warming. Since most scientists agree on the mainstream climate science, networks trying to host climate debates often pull media personalities, industry reps, or others to represent the counter side of the "climate debate." These people are usually much more skilled at one-liners, quick comebacks, and using powerful and emotional language to connect with the pubic, not to mention they're usually more comfortable in front of the cameras and spotlight given their lines of work. By contrast, scientists are often introverts by nature, who spend much of their time analyzing data, writing grants, and teaching in front of small classrooms. Scientists are also much more careful with their words, avoiding bold language and anything that could overstate the science. When you compound this with their reluctance to speak of "causes" and their over-eagerness to talk about uncertainty, you get a perfect storm in which mainstream climate scientists appear on shaky ground.

Two unfortunate scenarios arise from the public's confusion over uncertainty. The first is the obvious confusion and misinterpretation that comes from it, while the second is less innocent. Industry and others in power have strategically exploited this misunderstanding for personal gain. For instance, while many in the fossil fuel industry understand the scientific meaning of uncertainty (even having their own teams of scientists), they've nonetheless funded smear campaigns to attack climate science uncertainty in the media and elsewhere to confuse the public and policy makers. In his book *Don't Even Think About It*, George Marshall points out how former ExxonMobile CEO Rex Tillerson admits to believing the public is "illiterate in the areas of science, math, and engineering."[5] Tillerson then explains that interested parties take advantage of this ignorance to "manufacture fear" supported by "lazy and unhelpful media who are unwilling to do the homework." Well, now you know better than to fall for this trick!

16

Most Climate Studies Aren't Even About "Climate Science"

This concern was first brought to my attention during a recent visit to Capitol Hill, in which I had the opportunity to meet with my congressman to discuss climate change. My congressman happens to believe global warming is a hoax and is one of a dwindling few politicians to hold such an extreme view on the issue. We chatted for an entire half hour, during which I attempted to explain to him the ways in which some organizations deliberately cherry-pick information to create headlines that confuse the public about the climate science. An example I cited was a recent blurb I read that stated something to the effect of "51 studies this year alone refute the so-called climate consensus." Quite persuasive, right? After reading the blurb, I proceeded to do a quick database search for all "climate change" related studies. What did I find? About 1,500 total studies had been published that year. After some simple arithmetic, one finds that the whopping 51 studies equates to a mere 3% of the total. Interestingly, this mini analysis happened to agree remarkably well with the 97% climate consensus we discussed in Chapter 7!

After explaining this little anecdote to my congressman, he replied that most studies discussing climate change are not even about climate change per se, and therefore cannot be said to support the climate consensus. That is, most studies don't dive into the fundamentals of climate science, meaning the physics of greenhouse gases and the role of human activity and pollution emissions in present-day warming. Despite the 51 counter studies likely having issues of their own—perhaps being industry-funded attempts to confuse the public and stall climate policy—the congressman was nonetheless right in his remarks. Most studies today don't focus on these fundamentals. So, why is that? The answer is simple.

Recall from Chapter 1 that the science on the greenhouse effect and the heat-trapping nature of CO_2 and other gases dates back to the 1800s when John Tyndall built his first chamber experiments and Svante Arrhenius first calculated the global warming impacts from doubling atmospheric CO_2. In other words, the fundamentals behind greenhouse gases, their warming effects, and the influence of human activity is old news.

Scientists don't tend to launch studies about old news. Similarly, science journals don't publish new studies that say what has already been said, unless the verdict is still out on a topic. And as we've already discussed, the verdict is *not* out on whether CO_2, methane, and other greenhouse gases warm the planet or whether humans are playing a role in the warming. It is understood and accepted by scientists. Most studies today focus on better understanding the impacts of climate change and the degree and timescale of expected warming. Hence, the congressman was right in asserting that most of today's climate studies don't focus directly on the fundamentals of climate science. However, it's only because the fundamentals are understood. So, why the "climate debate?" More on this in the next chapter.

17

There Is Still A "Climate Debate."
The Science Isn't Settled!

The notion of a climate change "debate" has been around for as long as I can remember, granted I'm not that old! However, in the ten or so years that I've been studying and following the issue, I have yet to actually encounter this so-called debate—at least not within the scientific community. Sure, I've spoken with non-scientist friends and others who have differing opinions on climate change. And we all know politicians can debate the issue until they're blue in the face. But I have yet to encounter a fellow scientist who rejects the fundamental notion that climate change is occurring, and that human activity is the primary cause. For most scientists, the evidence is simply too compelling.

Returning to this notion of a debate, one must then ask, who is doing the debating? And if scientists aren't the ones debating, do we really care? Should we even call it a debate? After all, climate change is rooted in science. Yet all too often people turn to politicians and neighbors for their opinions on climate change. Most politicians are unlikely to have ever taken a single course on climate science, atmospheric chemistry, glaciology or oceanography, let alone dedicated years to climate research. The same could be said for most peoples' friends and family. Yet these are the opinions on which most peoples' personal views of climate change are based. Surely you wouldn't turn to a politician or next-door neighbor for official medical or legal advice. You'd consult a physician and lawyer. For some reason, though, it's become all too common for people to turn to friends, family, and political figures for climate "advice." The extent to which scientists possess a unique expertise and understanding of the complex inner workings of the climate has seemingly been forgotten. And the media doesn't always do the best job of speaking on their behalf.

Most scientists accept the fundamental science of climate change and have moved on to more pressing questions. How much will the climate warm? How quickly can we slow climate change if we cut carbon emissions in half? How much will sea level rise by the end of the century? These are but a few of the questions scientists are now asking. "Is climate change real?" and "Are humans the cause?" are questions that were answered decades ago and are no longer interesting to pursue for most scientists.

Since climate change is a scientific issue that nearly every scientist agrees on, it is reasonable to ask why the phrase "climate debate" still gets tossed around. The answer is multifaceted and has more to do with science communication than science itself. It also involves a dark side. That is, strategic deception and engineered confusion by industry. Most people don't realize it, but the first major scientific efforts to seriously study climate change were launched by a company that has ironically become one of the leading propagators of "climate denial" information—none other than Exxon Mobile (then called Exxon).

According to an investigative report recently published by *Inside Climate News*, Exxon's knowledge of climate change and the threat of carbon dioxide emissions dates back at least to the 1970s, when one of its senior scientists, James F. Black, explained the risks to a team of company leaders.[6] Exxon at first responded responsibly, launching an ambitious program to measure and monitor CO_2 levels as well as model the climate. This even included outfitting a supertanker with custom-made instruments to sample CO_2 in the air and ocean. According to the report, by 1982 research had led the head of theoretical science at Exxon Corporate Research Laboratories to conclude that a doubling of CO_2 in the atmosphere would warm the globe by about 3°C, enough to bring about "significant changes in Earth's climate."

Within a decade the pro-climate science mood of the company would change as company leaders began to diverge from the message of their scientists. Exxon slashed funding to many of its climate change research programs by more than half, and instead began a smear campaign to cast doubt on the very climate science its own research team had helped to conduct. Rather than continuing to advance the world's understanding of global warming, the company instead lobbied to block federal and international action to control greenhouse gas emissions. Recently, researchers at Harvard examined nearly 200 climate change communications from Exxon between 1977 and 2014, including peer-reviewed and non-peer-reviewed publications, internal company documents, and paid, editorial-style advertisements.[7] After a thorough content analysis, the authors of the study concluded that Exxon "misled the public" about climate change.

Our story about Exxon highlights the role corruption has played in confusing the public and engineering doubt about climate science. By deriding their own scientists and overstating the uncertainties of climate models and measurements, Exxon strategically helped paint the picture of a "climate debate." If left alone, this strategy may not have succeeded. However, factors relating to science communication provided the necessary kindling to fuel the "debate." This is where the second piece of the puzzle comes in.

Although scientists work hard, their work usually takes the form of highly technical analyses that the public never reads. Unless you're in school, this means that the job of communicating science to the public falls on the media—newspapers, websites, and T.V. programs. This could be fine and dandy if science was simple. But often times it's not. And news reporters don't always do the best jobs of interpreting studies and relaying important information to their audiences.

Additionally, media outlets, while valuable sources of news, are businesses at the end of the day. That is, they operate with earnings in mind. For a newspaper or television network, earnings are generated by running advertisements (newspaper spreads, commercials, etc.). When reporting the news, media outlets are therefore careful to avoid coverage that will turnoff client advertisers. One group of heavy-weight hitters that spends hundreds of millions each year on advertising is the fossil fuel industry. In the case of climate change, it would be naive to think their deep pockets and advertising power have played no role in the general absence of televised climate change coverage over the years. One major news network has taken it even further, using its platform to outright reject the notion of human-caused global warming.

Let's expand a bit further on the media. It's important to distinguish between things that are equal and things that are simply represented equally in the news. While most scientists and scientific bodies including the Intergovernmental Panel on Climate Change, the National Academy of Sciences, and others all agree that human activity is causing climate change, industry think tanks have brilliantly exploited the journalistic tendency towards "balanced" reporting, which has resulted in the industry view, supported only by a minority of scientists, receiving nearly equal coverage when compared to the mainstream climate science consensus. This disproportionate reporting, which assigns equal coverage to the counterargument against climate change, has created the illusion of a debate, when in fact there is *no* debate. This has had the devastating effect of confusing the public and policymakers. The benefit to industry is that more confusion equals less action, meaning fewer policies that would require industry to control its pollution emissions.

Another reason for the "climate debate" has to do with television entertainment. How many times have you raced home to catch a live-streamed "agreement" on television? Probably never! That's because agreements aren't entertaining and don't make for good T.V. Instead, networks televise debates. Even on issues as scientifically agreed upon as climate change, T.V. networks will nonetheless find one person to argue one side of the issue and another to give the counterargument. As with "balanced reporting," this tragically misleads the public into believing that scientists are equally divided on the issue. In actuality, over 90% of scientists writing about climate change or global warming agree that climate change is occurring and caused by humans. Were networks more concerned with reflecting the *consensus* rather than creating good entertainment and simply showing "both sides," they might consider recruiting a panel of nine scientists to speak to the climate consensus, and a single scientist to voice the counterargument. How's that for a debate?!

18

Temperature And CO_2 Are Within The Range Of Natural Variation

This phrase has been echoed by the leading voices of climate change skepticism, including some of the most organized and well-funded campaigns to undermine the climate consensus. What makes this claim particularly powerful to the denial campaign, unlike other claims, is that it is not actually false. In fact, it can even be broadened to include observed changes in snowfall, ice flow speed, glacial extent, and iceberg degradation. All these phenomena are occurring within the range of *natural* variability. How is this so? Simple. Earth is 4.5 billion years old. Scientists can reconstruct its temperature record going back for at least 65 million years. That's a BIG chunk of time! Over this period, Earth's climate has indeed been through dramatic swings, even more dramatic than today. However, this should be of no comfort to us. Earth has experienced some extreme—dare I say apocalyptic—climates in the past. Let's take a glimpse at the darker side of Earth's paleoclimate.

Around 700 million years ago, Earth was not as we know it today. In fact, far from it. Earth was in a frigid climatic state that scientists refer to as "snowball Earth." During this Cryogenian period, Earth was mostly frozen at its surface from the North Pole to the South Pole, extending all the way through the equator.[8] This was not the green and blue planet we've all come to know and love. From outer space, it would've resembled something quite different. And this snowball period remained as such for about 10 million years. Evidence of Earth's snowball past comes from geological evidence of glaciers near the equator. If glaciers could have expanded all the way to the equator, the argument goes, then they must have covered the entire planet. Snowball Earth is thought to have been the result of a runaway cooling effect. In fact, evidence suggests that Earth underwent at least two such snowball periods in its history.

Let's turn to another extreme in Earth's paleoclimate, this time going some 50 million years back—just after the age of the dinosaurs. During this period, Earth was very warm. So warm, in fact, that the North and South Pole were devoid of ice, and crocodiles and palm trees flourished beyond the Arctic Circle. With the absence of polar ice sheets, the oceans of this so-called "hot house" Earth contained much more water. Sea levels were consequently higher than today by a staggering 300 meters, or nearly 1,000 feet! Put another way, the oceans were sufficiently high to submerge about one-third of the present-day land surface. Given that the majority of the world's current population lives within 100 miles of the coast, one can only imagine what this would have meant to modern civilization. How does all *this* sound for "natural variation?"

The climatic extremes of Earth's history are important to bear in mind, not for the sake of fear, but because it's important to understand the climates of Earth's past if we're to truly appreciate the mild climate of today. In contrast to past extremes, the climate that accompanied the sharp expansion of human civilization over the last 10,000 years has been relatively warm and remarkably stable. Such stability has meant relatively stable snow cover, sea level, and seasonal weather. It's this extended period of climatic stability to which we owe much thanks for the success of human civilization.

Prior to our mild climate, humans had been mostly a nomadic species, dependent on hunter-gather practices. With the stability of Earth's climate around 11,000 years ago—known as the Holocene period—came a transition to farming and, with more successful techniques, a vast increase in the production of extra food. This allowed the emergence of permanent settlements such as villages, towns, and ultimately cities. The stable climate benefited farming through predictable weather, water supplies, and other environmental factors. Climatic stability also meant stable sea levels, leading to reliable fishing and shellfishing grounds that provided early humans with a high-protein marine diet, as well as allowed for grain production in estuary and floodplain ecosystems. Known as the Neolithic revolution, the sudden transition to permanent settlements and abundant food resulted in increased innovation of stone tools and other items as well as community structure, thus setting the stage for society as we know it.

The climate stability of the Holocene sustained itself within about 1°C throughout the greater part of human society, from ancient times to the modern era—that is, until now. In less than 150 years, global average temperature has already risen by another one degree Cesius.[9] Human activity beginning around the industrial revolution, and more so in recent decades, has caused this climatic destabilization. According to James Hansen, former director of NASA's Goddard Institute for Space Studies, global temperatures as of 2000 reached approximately as high as at any prior time during the entire 11,000-year Holocene period. Temperatures since have only begun to break record highs. In fact, based on the 138-year temperature record of the National Oceanic and Atmospheric Administration, the top ten warmest years on record all occurred within the last two decades, with the top three hottest years on record being 2015, 2016, and 2017.[10] This is a foreboding trend that ought to concern us.

As we've seen, the climate on Earth has not always been so stable, but has instead seen extremes that have swung it from hothouse to snowball phases. Talk of "natural variation" should therefore not comfort us. At issue is not whether present day warming is within the limits of natural variation. Of course it is! Earth is too old and has seen far too much. But "natural" cannot be taken to mean "harmless," especially for humans. What is at issue is whether humanity and society as we know it can *cope* with such variation, particularly as our agriculture, freshwater supplies, and coastal communities come under increased threat from severe storms, drought, and sea level rise. Exacerbating such impacts and our ability to cope is the short timespan over which temperatures are rising. Even in Earth's history, temperature extremes were usually drawn out over thousands and even millions of years. However, global warming today is occurring rapidly, on the order of centuries and even decades. This is a radical change, even compared to Earth's dramatic past.

Though probably obvious by now, there is a final point worth making. Saying that present-day warming is within the range of natural variation is not the same as saying present-day warming is "natural." This is an important distinction. Climate drivers of the past may have been natural and produced warmer temperatures than today. But the climate drivers of the past are the climate drivers of the past. Human activity didn't exist back then to influence the climate. Today of course, the situation is different. Earth's natural climate drivers are still at play. However, it's the influence of human activity that has become the predominant driving force behind climate change. While the past is still informative, we must bear in mind that humans inhabit the present and should therefore not let our thinking get overly boxed in by the natural drivers of Earth's paleoclimate.

Furthermore, recalling that humans adapted to the climate of Earth's very recent past, which was mild, climate drivers and temperature levels from millions of years ago should only be of limited interest to us. Importantly, humans weren't around to experience Earth's natural paleoclimatic extremes. The success of our species and modern society has therefore not been tested against major swings in Earth's climate. So, while we should be interested in where temperatures and climates have been, we should be most interested and even concerned about where they go from here.

19

CO_2 Can't Be Measured With Precision

It's probably fair to say that this claim has been most widely circulated lately by none other than our own recent U.S. Environmental Protection Agency administrator—Scott Pruitt. While having ironically presided over a mostly science-based agency, Pruitt was notorious for his rejection of mainstream climate science and the notion that CO_2 is warming the atmosphere. He is often quoted as saying that carbon dioxide cannot be measured with sufficient "precision" to support the climate consensus. Well, is this true?

First, by "precision" I think we must assume that Pruitt actually means "accuracy." These terms are often confused. Precision is the ability to measure something repeatedly and get similar results each time. CO_2 sensors are indeed precise. I've used them myself! If they didn't produce similar results from one minute or hour to the next, no scientist would waste money purchasing them for his or her laboratory. And as it turns out, CO_2 sensors take new readings not every minute or hour, but anywhere from 20 times a second to twice per minute. With each new reading the instrumental software takes into account previous measurements and reports an average—thus solving any problems of precision.

To the question of accuracy, this can be experimentally tested and demonstrated. By releasing a known amount of pure CO_2 into a fixed volume of air, scientists can easily use a pen and paper to calculate the CO_2 concentration. At this point, all that's left to do is stick the CO_2 sensor in the fixed volume and see how well the CO_2 measurement stacks up against the calculated *true* concentration. There you go, simple as that! And if the sensor is inaccurate, you can simply adjust it to match the true concentration, a process known as calibration. You can also do "zero" calibration, in which a sensor is placed in a gas-free chamber and adjusted to give a zero reading. This is the same concept you use when you calibrate your bathroom scale to make sure it displays a zero when nobody is weighing themselves. Calibration is routinely carried out for all types of instruments to ensure their accuracy prior to use. In the case of CO_2 in a normal outdoor setting, sensors are extremely accurate. The NOAA Earth System Research Laboratory, for instance, collects CO_2 measurements at its Mauna Loa Observatory that are accurate within about 0.2 ppm.[11] Given that today's global CO_2 level is around 410 ppm, this corresponds to an accuracy of over 99.9%!

20

Scientists Are Just Defending Their Work!

Earlier I mentioned a conversation I had with my congressman last year. During that interesting chat, I was surprised to learn that my congressman truly believed climate change to be nothing more than a wild theory, or the "CO_2 theory" as he put it with a rather dismissive roll of the eyes. Among other things, the congressman suggested that many climate scientists were hotshots with big egos, who would rather propagate a false theory than admit they were wrong. This comment of course neglects the fact that empirical evidence has thus far *supported*, not *refuted*, mainstream climate science—CO_2 accumulating, temperatures going up, oceans rising, glaciers melting, hurricanes becoming more intense, etc. Nonetheless, the congressman went on to describe the so-called climate consensus as essentially a bunch of science friends "deciding to agree" about climate change, as if it had occurred over a couple of beers at the neighborhood pub. At this point, it was evident that the congressman possessed little understanding of the nature and inner-workings of science and research. Though disturbed to hear such a sinister view of science coming from a person of his stature and power, it's only safe to assume he is not alone in his perspective. Let's therefore consider his comments.

To the notion of "egos," it's true that even scientists can succumb to stubbornness about various hypotheses and viewpoints, especially older scientists who may have invested an entire career to a particular line of research. As discussed in Chapter 1, science about the greenhouse effect and global warming dates back to the nineteenth century. There is nothing *new* about the heat trapping properties of CO_2, methane, and other greenhouse gases. For those unconvinced, you can watch greenhouse gas experiments online or do one yourself. What's *new* is a growing public awareness about the science, rather than the science itself. Of course, there are always new studies coming out that build upon prior work, but the underlying fundamentals of climate science have been around for over a century. This is important to recognize because it means the scientists who first cooked up the "CO_2 theory" have long passed away, taking their egos with them. Those who carried the climate torch upon their passing have long passed on too. While a couple of stubborn scientists may be enough to keep an idea alive, it's not enough to keep it alive through generations of future scientists. Today, climate science has become a heavily researched and interdisciplinary field, involving oceanographers, glaciologist, atmospheric physicists, ecologists, and geologists, from various universities and agencies across the entire world. It is not a fringe science kept alive by a stubborn few who are trying to save face.

Along the theme of *ego*, it's also worth noting that a great deal of scientists are young up-and-comers like myself who have yet to establish revolutionary theories or publish breakthrough studies. We're merely professionals with an expertise in science and experimentation. Young researchers therefore don't carry the big egos that come with some senior scientists, and therefore have little to *defend* and little at stake. Incidentally, these same young scientists are the ones who sift through the climate data and carry out most of the monotonous analyses that lead to the climate studies we often hear about. The notion of a sea of "hot shots" propagating a faltered theory simply doesn't hold up.

As far as the climate consensus and notion of benevolent agreement and comradery, most scientists would find this laughable. It's not because scientists aren't friendly or never agree. It's because scientists are extremely skeptical and require a high burden of proof to become convinced of something, not to mention are extremely critical of each other's work. In other words, they don't just "buy" what they hear, and are generally conservative in their claims. This turns out to be a useful quality for a scientist. After all, science is about asking questions and finding answers through evidence. Where no evidence exists, no answers can be claimed. When scientists make claims based on little or no evidence, they set themselves up to be proven wrong by other scientists willing to put in the extra effort to get to the bottom of the research question. This makes for an embarrassing situation that can tarnish one's credibility. Scientists are therefore careful to avoid making claims or buying into a hypothesis when sufficient evidence is lacking. Similarly, they don't just agree to agree. Evidence is crucial. This is always the guiding light in science.

It's worth pausing and recapping to let this sink in. Scientists don't jump to conclusions without sound evidence. It's a risk to their credibility, reputation, and career. They're also inherently skeptical and critical of each other's work. Now let's un-pause and reflect on the present issue of climate change. Despite these barriers, scientists from around the world accept climate change as a serious problem that is a result of human activity and are sounding an alarm for society to take action. They are clearly and confidently describing the underlying causes of climate change and identifying solutions such as alternative energy that can help curb greenhouse gas emissions and arrest the warming crisis. They are also describing the undeniable consequences that will result from inaction, many of which are already starting to occur. In many cases, scientists, including myself, are even stepping into the unfamiliar world of advocacy to get the message across.[12] It is rare for scientists to be so collectively clear, concerned, and vocal about an issue. Such mobilization should cause politicians and the public to go into very high alert.

Having emphasized the competitive nature of science, it's also worth mentioning that the dream of any scientist is to receive that holy grail known as a Nobel Prize. This prestigious award is reserved only for scientists who make truly revolutionary breakthroughs and discoveries. Having said that, let's play devil's advocate for a minute and say that man-made climate change is just a bunch of mumbo jumbo. An up-and-coming scientist like myself would gain a whole lot more recognition and be a whole lot closer to wining a Nobel Prize if they could *disprove* mainstream climate science, as opposed to simply publishing one more study to sit atop the mountain of other climate consensus studies. Think about that. Demonstrating that the climate ISN'T changing or that humans AREN'T the cause would be a sure ticket to fame, not to mention earn you a lot of new friends who were previously depressed over the issue. Thus, if there were holes in mainstream climate science, you can bet they'd have been jumped on and pursued instantly by opportunistic up-and-comers. Unfortunately, such holes are hard to find.

Nonetheless, there *are* a few scientists who have taken this contrarian approach. It's unclear if the temptation for stardom was their motivation, or funding by industry, but the outcome is certain. This group of scientists is in high demand, getting called in for frequent radio interviews, guest lectures, climate debates, and even authoring books. Meanwhile, the remaining 97% of climate scientists experience little fame and fortune. In the case of climate change, it literally pays to be a contrarian. There is only one drawback—a lack of evidence to support the contrarian perspective. Without this critical piece—evidence—the majority of climate scientists will likely continue working for relatively low pay and little glamor. After all, most scientists didn't enter the field for fame and fortune (a real shocker right?), but rather to study and improve our understanding of the world.

21

How Can We Predict Next Year's Climate When We Can Hardly Predict Next Week's Weather?

This is a fair question. I can certainly recall many an "Armageddon" storm that became little more than a few raindrops. And most of us can recall our fair share of sunny forecasts that left us on a chilly beachside. The misnomer in the question posed above doesn't have to do with the difficulty of predicting the weather. It's certainly a difficult task, and forecasters often get it wrong, especially five or ten days out. Rather, the issue is the distinction between "weather" and "climate." They are not the same. This is a common oversight that people on both sides of the climate issue are guilty of making. All too often people reference the *weather* as either evidence supporting or refuting the notion of global warming. However, weather events in and of themselves cannot refute or prove climate change. We must stick to the *climate* data for that.

So, what's the difference between climate and weather? *Weather* is what you experience when you wake up in the morning and go to bed at night. It's that hot day in mid-July and that frigid morning in February. That is, it's the dramatic fluctuations you observe in a single day and even over weeks and seasons. *Climate*, on the other hand, is the average of all that noisy weather activity, usually taken over 30-year periods. Consequently, the *climate* of a region is much more stable than its *weather.* Therefore, when scientists attempt to model and predict the climate, they're not trying to predict what the temperature will be like in Los Angeles on June 30th of 2036 (although hopefully perfect since it'll be my 50th birthday!). Rather, they're estimating what the *average* weather will be like over that general time period. This turns out to be a much easier task—albeit still highly sophisticated and involved.

To make predictions about the future climate, scientists need to consider a whole host of different environmental factors. How much energy does CO_2 absorb? How does ocean evaporation change as temperatures rise? How will ocean circulations change with changes in freshwater runoff? Considering this spiderweb of factors and how they each feed into and affect one another is not easy business for the human brain. Hence, computer models come into play! To create a model for predicting the climate, scientists must first tell the model everything they know about the climate system and key factors that influence it. This means inputting information about evaporation, cloud formation, greenhouse gas behavior, wind circulation, and other physical processes that are well-established and understood. Using mathematics and the fundamental laws of physics, fluid motion, and chemistry, scientists can then simulate the transfer of energy and materials between the air, water, and land, and gain a good understanding of climatic responses.

With present-day climate change, we're particularly interested in knowing how increases in greenhouse gas levels will continue to influence air temperature, precipitation, storms, etc. But what good are the models if we don't even know how well they predict? Do we really have to wait a decade or two to find out if they work? Fortunately not. To evaluate their performance, scientists can do what they call "hindcasting." You guessed it—the opposite of forecasting! In the absence of future data to compare climate predictions, it's practical to assess models using data from the past. Basically, we can just choose a past time point, let's say 1957, input the climatic conditions that existed then, and let the model go to work in predicting "future" conditions. Of course, it's not really the future bring predicted, but rather the future relative to our starting point (so perhaps the 1958-1970 "future"). In this way, scientist can conveniently compare predictions with actual temperature, precipitation, and other observations to assess model accuracy. This process is known as cross-validation and is standard practice across all types of modeling disciplines, including my own—air pollution exposure modeling!

Now that you've passed Climate Modeling 101, we can examine the question of whether and how well scientists can actually model and predict the climate. Let's take a look at some real-world climate models to see how their predictions have stacked up with real observations over time. There are a number of sophisticated models created by teams of scientists from around the world. Several have been around long enough for us to actually assess their performance using real data from years that have elapsed since their creation.

Let's look at the so-called Hansen model developed in 1988 by a team of NASA and MIT scientists led by then-NASA scientist James Hansen. In comparing temperature predictions made by the Hansen model with real-world observations, one finds that the model did a great job of forecasting the temperature trend. A quite serendipitous opportunity to quality-check the model arose when Mount Pinatubo in the Philippines decided to erupt in 1991. As we discussed in Chapter 3, volcanoes release large amounts of sulfur dioxide gas into the atmosphere, which ultimately turns into light reflecting particles. With this in mind, we'd expect the massive Pinatubo eruption to reflect sunlight and cause a slight cooling of Earth's climate. As it turns out, that's just what happened! The planet cooled by just under 1°F (about 0.5°C) for nearly three years. So, how well did the Hanson model predict this? Remarkably well. The model not only predicted the temperature drop accurately, but also the various feedback processes relating to water vapor and radiative effects.

Turning to the Intergovernmental Panel on Climate Change (IPCC). In its first assessment report in 1990, IPCC drew from a number of climate models to form a prediction relating to future sea level rise. Their central estimate was a value of about 2 millimeters per year of rise in the near future. As time would elapse, a comparison of actual rise with the IPCC predictions showed the true amount of sea rise to be about 3.4 millimeters per year. This corresponded with the worst-case scenario estimate outlined in the report. The IPCC report also used models to formulate estimates about the rate of future glacial melting. In this case, the rate of true melting outpaced the IPCC projections by about 40%. In short, models don't always get it perfectly right. But so far, they have tended to err on the side of being too conservative.

In his book *Climate Casino*, Yale economist William Nordhaus provides an in-depth discussion of climate models and the importance of integrated assessment models.[13] These models essentially allow for more comprehensive simulations that include not only climate dynamics, but other aspects of the science and economics of climate change as well. For instance, how will economic growth and policy measures influence CO_2 emissions? In assessing a variety of climate models, including his own, Williams highlights that projections of CO_2 emissions for the end of the century range from 1.6 to 5.4 times higher than 2000 levels, with the differences primarily lying in uncertainty about the rate of future global economic growth. He notes that resolving such uncertainty is simply not possible, and therefore that reliably predicting the future will always entail an element of unknown. However, rather than waiting until we can *know more*, he points out that "for climate change, waiting for the right answer is a perilous course. It is like driving 100 miles an hour with your headlights off on a foggy night and hoping there are no curves."

Fortunately, there are different teams of scientists from around the world who have developed different sophisticated climate models. One way of identifying reasonable climate predictions is to look at all the different estimates made by these various models. By evaluating them collectively, and taking an *average* of model predictions, scientists can provide a more robust estimate of climate-related impacts in the future. Moreover, the range of predictions by various models serve as useful best- and worst-case boundaries as it relates to future scenarios. Thus, climate models are not only feasible, but are quite powerful, particularly when considered in tandem. They can provide us with an important glimpse into the future, which better situates us to adapt to climate impacts as well as recognize the importance of immediate steps to reduce greenhouse gas emissions.

22

Warming Is Due To The Urban Heat Island Effect

For those unfamiliar, the "heat island" effect is the buildup of heat that often occurs in urban settings. Have you ever felt that burst of heat when walking across a black asphalt parking lot on a hot summer day? Well that's one component of the heat island effect. Black surfaces tend to absorb rather than reflect light. Consequently, they're usually hotter to the touch when exposed to sunlight. In cities and other urban settings where green vegetation and dirt have been largely replaced by black roads, paved parking lots, and tar roofs, this added heat retention can add up. When you combine this with an abundance of tall buildings, which can reduce wind and natural ventilation, and the presence of factories and automobiles, which release hot exhaust into the air, the result is a buildup of heat around urban areas. Taken together, these combined factors create what we call the "heat island effect."

So, what does this have to do with climate change? Since

many meteorological stations are located in urban areas, there are some who like to claim the increase in global average temperatures we've observed in recent decades is merely reflecting local temperature rises that are due to greater urbanization and stronger heat island effects, rather than the greenhouse effect. At first glance, this claim admittedly sounds reasonable. However, it grossly underestimates the understanding of the scientific community about the work they conduct, and the steps scientists take to ensure data is not biased.

Knowledge of the urban heat island effect is not new and is probably one reason meteorologists tend to locate their monitoring stations away from heat island centers, instead opting for nearby green spaces, hilltops, and parks. This minimizes temperature distortions that may arise from heat islands. The monitoring station for my graduate school department at Harvard, for instance, was located on the rooftop of our six-story library. This ensured higher wind ventilation and minimal influence of vehicle- and asphalt-related heat. And since we were measuring air pollution, it also ensured minimal influence of local car exhaust, so as not to bias our measurements. When scientists are trying to assess averages over widespread areas, they usually plan carefully to avoid local affects that could distort the data.

In addition to careful planning and data collection, scientists are also able to account for the heat island effect when it does occur. This is made possible because, in addition to urban stations, many rural meteorological stations exist. Rural areas of course don't act as heat islands. Therefore, scientists can compare urban and rural temperature trends over time and discern whether urban measurements were statistically higher. Interestingly, the difference is often negligibly small. Both urban areas and rural areas have been experiencing similar warming trends around the globe. In fact, one of the regions experiencing the greatest increases in temperature over recent decades is the North Pole, which is NOT an urban heat island.

23

Climate Models Don't Account For The Most Abundant Greenhouse Gas—Water Vapor!

L ike many misconceptions surrounding climate change, this statement carries a mix of both truth and fallacy. To the first part of the claim, climate models do indeed account for water vapor. If they didn't, it'd be hard to forecast the climate with any reasonable accuracy. This is the part of the statement that rings false. The reason the accusation arises, however, is because people are looking in the wrong places. Water vapor is not considered a climate "forcing" factor, like carbon dioxide, methane, and sulfate aerosols. Therefore, it's not labeled alongside these other factors when scientists describe their models in written manuscripts and reports. Water vapor is instead considered a "feedback," which is quite different. Climate forcing factors are essentially defined as the initial drivers of the climate, whereas feedbacks are processes that amplify those initial drivers (either positively or negatively).

The reason water vapor is not considered a climate forcing factor is because atmospheric water vapor levels mostly *respond* to changes in climate, rather than *cause* them. Human activity, for instance, cannot readily affect global water vapor concentrations in the atmosphere. Rather, vapor levels are dictated by temperature. As the planet warms, more evaporation takes place. Interestingly, warmer air can hold more water. The result is that warmer atmospheres contain more water vapor. The reason water vapor is considered a feedback is because water vapor is a greenhouse gas, which can amplify temperature changes when they occur. (See Climate Change 101 for examples of other important climate feedbacks.) But because the temperature change must occur first, water vapor is only a feedback and not a forcing factor. Let's elaborate on water vapor's role as a greenhouse gas.

It is true that water vapor is a powerful greenhouse gas—and even the most abundant greenhouse gas. That is, water vapor accounts for about 1% of the atmosphere, compared to only 0.04% for CO_2. Because water vapor is a greenhouse gas, and because its atmospheric levels rise and fall with temperature, water vapor can serve as an important feedback that can amplify the effects of other factors—thus leading to more extreme changes in temperature. The reason water vapor concentrations are so tightly tied to temperature is because at some point cloud formation and precipitation occur. That is, vapor can only accumulate so much at a given temperature before the atmosphere ultimately becomes saturated and the vapor begins to condense into droplets that just fall out (rain). Let's look at an example for clarity.

If we take a hypothetical globe that's at a stable temperature, we can safely assume that the amount of evaporation from the oceans, lakes, and land is roughly equal to the amount of precipitation that falls back down. Even if we try and pump a bunch of extra water vapor into the air, our ability to create more greenhouse warming will be limited because the atmosphere is already saturated with water and can't take up much more. The added vapor would therefore mostly condense and fall out as rain. Similarly, due to the abundance of oceans, if we tried to vacuum all of the water out of the atmosphere, it would be quickly replaced through evaporation. Thus, although water vapor is a strong greenhouse gas, we can't really change its abundance in the atmosphere. Therefore, it's role in climate change is limited. That is, until we manage to tinker with Earth's temperature dial, water vapor levels remain stable. Once the heat is turned up, however, the atmosphere's capacity to store water increases, at which point water vapor levels can rise and begin to wreak additional warming havoc, driving temperatures further up. Because water vapor cannot *initiate* such temperature changes, but only *amplify* them when they occur, it is not considered a climate forcing factor.

By the way, this feedback dynamic can work in the opposite direction. Since cooler air can store less water vapor, turning down the heat means water vapor condenses out of the air. (This is why droplets of morning dew can be spotted outside after temperatures have fallen overnight!) With less water vapor in the air, there is less greenhouse warming. Thus, temperatures drop even further. Again, for this dynamic to kick in, some other factors must first adjust the thermostat. Let's get to some not-so-hypothetical "other factors"—namely, carbon dioxide, methane, and other greenhouse gases—and consider water's role as a feedback, or amplifier, of their temperature influence.

In the case of CO_2, industrial activities and vehicle emissions have released more carbon into the air, which has allowed the atmosphere to trap more heat and increase temperatures. The same can be said for other important greenhouse gases such as methane and nitrous oxide from agricultural activities. By emitting such pollutants, we've got our "turning up" of the temperature dial. This is where water vapor is able to kick in and amplify the warming. CO_2 and our other gases lead to warming. Warming leads to more water vapor in the atmosphere. More water vapor leads to even more warming. Thus, we have our climate forcing factor and our feedback system at work. Getting back to the claim at the top of the chapter, water vapor is indeed an important greenhouse gas. However, due to the important reasons we've discussed, it is not a climate forcing factor and cannot be categorized alongside CO_2 and other greenhouse gases.

Water vapor's role as a temperature amplifier has major implications for our climate. According to a 2008 study out of Texas A&M University, positive feedback from water vapor is sufficient to double the climate warming caused by increased carbon dioxide.[14] The authors concluded that the "existence of a strong and positive water-vapor feedback means that projected business-as-usual greenhouse-gas emissions over the next century are virtually guaranteed to produce warming of several degrees Celsius." This yet again highlights the importance of taking immediate steps to reduce our greenhouse gas emissions.

24

Don't You Know
The Sun Is Getting Brighter?

Being a so-called "main sequence" star, the sun is indeed expanding and getting brighter as its core density increases. But is this the reason for historic climate change and recent warming? A quick look at the recent paleoclimate record will remind us that temperatures on Earth have swung up and down about every hundred thousand years. They haven't followed a simple upward path as the notion of an ever-growing sun would suggest. Similarly, temperatures today are rapidly on the rise, which is inconsistent with a *gradually* brightening sun. So, what's going on? For starters, the sun's expansion is VERY gradual.

To get a sense of how gradual the sun is brightening, consider that in its nearly five-billion-year lifetime the sun's luminosity has only increased by about 30%. This is about 1% every 160 million years. A 1% increase could certainly influence the climate, but only by about 2-4°F (around 1-2°C). This is far too small to have any meaningful impact on

117

the one or two century timescale that we're talking about. In the case of present-day climate change, we've seen a 1.3°F (0.7°C) increase in just 70 years, and will likely see another degree or more rise by the end of the century. Clearly, there are other forces at play.

Throughout Earth's history, the reason temperatures haven't followed a simple upward path is because there are other planetary phenomena that overshadow the influence of the sun's very gradual expansion. The Milankovitch cycles described in Chapter 4 are examples of factors that play a much greater role in influencing the Earth's climate than solar expansion. Even the sun's own decadal solar cycles and changes in sunspot activity turn out to influence the climate more than its growth in size (See Chapter 5). Solar expansion is simply not the answer.

25

We Breathe Out CO$_2$, So How Bad Can It Be?

It's correct that humans and other animals exhale carbon dioxide—yes, the same carbon dioxide involved in the climate crisis. So, why all the fuss? First, cars and power plants "exhale" a whole lot more CO$_2$ than humans by burning fossil fuels. A look at the transportation sector alone can demonstrate this. Each day, the typical person exhales around 2-3 lbs of carbon dioxide. By comparison, the tailpipe of a typical passenger vehicle releases this much in just 3-4 miles of driving.[15] Considering the average American drives over 13,000 miles each year, one can quickly see that there is no comparison here!

In addition to powering our cars, fossil fuels are also burned to produce electricity, heat our homes, propel airplanes, etc. Globally, these activities combined release over 10,000 lbs of CO$_2$ per person into the air each year.[16] So yes, as humans we do produce our own CO$_2$. But it's negligible compared to the carbon-intensive activities we engage in. And we haven't even accounted for non-CO_2 greenhouse gases that we emit through agriculture and other processes. The comparison here is reminiscent of Chapter 3 when we compared the CO_2 released by volcanoes versus that released by human activity. The "human" volcano was a whole lot larger!

Though our comparison was insightful, there's a reason we didn't even need to bother with it. Animals have long exhaled carbon dioxide. When this carbon gets exhaled, it floats off into the air. Some gets absorbed by plants, some dissolves into the oceans, some makes its way into the soils, and some remains in the air. This dynamic process of carbon moving throughout the environment is known as the carbon cycle. Importantly, this cycle is in a state of what scientists call "equilibrium," meaning the amount of carbon entering and exiting any of these environmental compartments at any given time is roughly the same. This means that carbon dioxide exhaled by animals doesn't *add* to the overall CO_2 in the system, because it is literally *part* of the system. As animals eat plants and release the carbon as CO_2 into the air, new plants grow and pull that CO_2 back out. So there's no net change in total atmospheric carbon. In short, the carbon we exhale is the same carbon we "inhale" from the atmosphere by the plants we eat. Even when we consume meat, the carbon originates from plants that the livestock fed on.

The carbon cycle as I've described it is the carbon cycle we've known throughout most of human history. However, today we find ourselves in a different situation. We have taken this happily balanced cycle and monkeyed with it. In addition to cutting down trees and thus removing carbon from the "biosphere compartment," we have also introduced *new* carbon into the system—and a LOT of it! That is, we've reached literally thousands of feet underground, into the most remote and isolated pockets of the Earth, to liberate prehistoric stores of oil and gas. Similarly, we've carved into hillsides and blown the tops off mountains to uncover coal. Fossil fuels are called "fossil" for a reason. They've taken millions of years to form—all the while remaining locked beneath the surface, at a comfortable distance from the air and the carbon cycle. By bringing this carbon to the surface, and subsequently burning it, as we've done in recent centuries, we've essentially poured excess carbon (in the form of CO_2) into an otherwise stable system; thus, upsetting the balance.

The most immediate result of dumping this new carbon into the air is of course to increase atmospheric CO_2 levels. However, it doesn't stop there. With more CO_2 in the air, the carbon cycle needs to find a new balance. This means increased levels of carbon entering the oceans, soils, and—where possible—the biosphere (plants). The absorption of carbon dioxide by these other environmental compartments has been a huge help in that the atmosphere has been spared what would have otherwise been an even greater increase in CO_2 levels. Thus, temperatures have not gone up as much as they would have otherwise. However, it's bad in other ways.

Probably the best example of the "bad" side has to do with the oceans. Atmospheric carbon dioxide dissolves into the oceans and other water bodies to form carbonic acid. More CO_2 therefore means a lower pH for ocean waters (more acidic). The shift to more acidic oceans is having a devastating impact on marine ecosystems, particularly in the equatorial waters that support our spectacular coral reefs. Acid makes it more difficult for coral to maintain its hard calcium carbonate structures. Hence, coral is becoming weakened and even vulnerable to destruction caused by turbulent storms. Should reefs wither away and cease to dissipate wave energy (one of their important functions), many coastlines will be at increased risk from erosion and damage, particularly during episodes of intense weather and storm surge.

Just as Earth has a carbon equilibrium, it also has an energy equilibrium. As the atmosphere heats up, some of this heat energy gets taken up by the oceans. In this way, coral reefs are experiencing a double whammy. Warmer oceans are not boding well for these delicate creatures, which already live in the warmest oceans of the world. As ocean temperatures increase, coral "bleaching" and ultimate coral death are becoming widespread among reefs. In 2016, a major warming episode led to a *New York Post* headline that read, "Great Barrier Reef dead at 25 million."[17] While the headline was exaggerated, an estimated 30% of this global treasure did in fact die in what was considered the worst mass "bleaching" event on record. (See Chapter 46 for more on *bleaching*).[18] In some areas, up to 80% of the reef sustained severe bleaching with over half of the coral ultimately perishing.[19] Once dead, coral reefs have a difficult time recovering. In many cases, they transform into what resemble barren wastelands consumed by algae and sea urchins. The demise of coral reefs is troubling beyond pure beauty and aesthetics when we consider that hundreds of millions of people depend on reef fish for their protein.

Let's get back to atmospheric carbon. Sure, we have all of this new CO_2 entering the atmosphere, but how do we *know* it's due to human activity and fossil fuel burning. The mathematician will tell you it's because we know how much carbon we're burning and can calculate the resulting CO_2 output and impact on global CO_2 concentrations. While that's true, let's look at another means of proof. Remember our cool science lesson on elemental isotopes from Chapter 2? Well as it turns out, the carbon atoms in plant matter (or fossil fuels, which are derived from ancient plants) are dominated by different carbon isotopes than regular CO_2 found in the atmosphere. When we burn forests or fossil fuels, these unique carbon isotopes therefore leave a sort of "signature" with the CO_2 molecules they release. Scientists can conveniently use this as an ID card to trace atmospheric carbon dioxide back to its source. When scientists carry out this analysis, they confirm that the modern increase in atmospheric CO_2 levels has indeed originated mostly from burning fossil fuels, which is what we'd expect.[20]

26

CO$_2$ Isn't Even Toxic!

True, carbon dioxide is not inherently toxic to health, at least not at normal levels, and is therefore not your typical "pollutant." This is why the gas remained unregulated by U.S. Environmental Protection Agency (EPA) under the Clean Air Act for so long. The only time CO$_2$ becomes "toxic" is when it builds up excessively in the indoor environment, which can happen in occupational settings (working in confined spaces) or when many people are stuffed in a crowded room with poor ventilation (since people exhale CO$_2$). Such high levels, however, are rare. In all but the most extreme cases, elevated CO$_2$ results in little more than headache or fatigue.

Importantly, toxicity and greenhouse gas potential are two quite different things. And carbon dioxide being of little health concern unfortunately doesn't take away from its potency as a greenhouse gas. It is because of its heat-trapping capacity and role in global warming that CO$_2$ has finally come under regulation as an air pollutant. Though relatively non-toxic, CO_2 is not innocent, and certainly poses a threat to health, even if the threat is indirect—as with climate change.

While we're on the topic of toxicity, it's well worth our time to point out some co-benefits of reducing CO_2 emissions. While carbon dioxide itself may not be toxic at ambient levels, it's partners in crime are the most toxic substances in our atmosphere. What do I mean? Well, the main anthropogenic (human-caused) sources of CO_2 emissions—cars and power plants—don't release CO_2 gas in isolation. When fossil fuels such as gasoline, coal, and oil are burned (for energy), they release all types of toxic air pollutants, including soot particles, nitrogen oxides, sulfur, mercury, iron, nickel, vanadium, and just about every other element on the periodic table. Coal plants even release small amounts of radioactive uranium and thorium into the air.[21] It's okay to live on a planet abundant with chemicals, but we don't want them all floating around in the air we breathe! It's better to keep them in the ground or in the laboratory.

Carbon dioxide's partner pollutants have been well studied for decades. Research on their health impacts picked up sharply after an extreme air pollution episode in London killed over 4,000 people in a single week of December 1952. Infamously known as the London Smog, this episode demonstrated for the first time the undeniable ability of air pollution to be not just a nuisance, but a cause of death. Less severe events around the same time in New York and Pennsylvania pointed to the same conclusion.

In the U.S., mounting concern of the impacts of air pollution led to the passage of the Clean Air Act of 1970 as well as numerous studies to better understand air pollution, its sources, and health effects. The most important of these was the so-called Harvard Six Cities Study which for the first time demonstrated scientifically a clear link between regular air pollution levels and life expectancy, using populations across six U.S. cities.[22] After accounting for age, gender, weight, whether people smoked cigarettes or not, plus other key factors, the cities with the greatest levels of air pollution showed substantially higher rates of mortality. The study linked the worst impacts to airborne particles—largely released by the burning of fossil fuels.

Today, air pollution is widely known to cause increased mortality as well as several adverse respiratory, cardiovascular, and even neurological conditions. Asthma in children, for instance, has been a major problem in urban areas with heavy vehicle traffic. Similarly, in cities where coal burning is high, people tend to have heart attacks and respiratory problems earlier in life. Heart attacks from air pollution? That's right. This puzzling-sounding connection is related to pollution-induced inflammation in the body, which causes constriction of the blood vessels, atherosclerotic plaques, among other problems.

All told, studies show that outdoor air pollution causes over 200,000 premature deaths in the U.S. each year, and a staggering 3.7 million deaths globally.[23,24] Air pollution coming from fossil fuels accounts for a substantial portion of this—and we're not even considering the other impacts from fossil fuels, including the water pollution and deforestation that comes with coal mining, fracking, and other processes.

On top of the impacts discussed so far, the International Agency for Research on Cancer, or IARC, announced in 2013 a re-classification of outdoor air pollution as a Group 1 human carcinogen.[25] A specialized cancer agency of the World Health Organization, IARC is a leading authority on the carcinogenicity of environmental chemicals. After a thorough review of what has amounted to decades of air pollution research and epidemiology, IARC officially concluded that there is "sufficient evidence that exposure to outdoor air pollution causes lung cancer." The group also noted a relationship between air pollution and an increased risk of bladder cancer.

While it's been understood for decades that air pollution leads to respiratory and cardiovascular diseases, a link with cancer has taken longer for scientists to demonstrate. Recent evidence, however, suggests that annually there are over 220,000 lung cancer deaths globally as a result of air pollution.[26] By officially characterizing outdoor air pollution as a human carcinogen, IARC is reminding us about the importance of reducing air pollution. The best way to do that? Burn less fossil fuel!

The sources that are polluting our communities with toxic chemicals are the same sources that are releasing climate-disrupting CO_2 into the air. The chemicals are released in tandem—a dirty mix—from smoke stacks, exhaust pipes, and even wood burning. While this is unfortunate, it also presents a great opportunity. It means that shifting away from fossil fuels to resolve climate change comes with a great deal of co-benefits to our health. By addressing climate change, we can address air pollution, reducing asthma, cardiovascular disease, cancers, and other diseases in the process. A win-win!

I've often wondered why scientists and climate advocates don't point out these co-benefits more often when trying to convince people of the need for climate action. I suppose it's because at the end of the day it's the greenhouse gases, not the toxic pollutants, that are responsible for the heat-trapping aspect of global warming. But given my own research specialization in toxic air pollution, I can't help but highlight these glaring co-benefits. In a 2011 Harvard study, the true cost of coal was quantified. The study meticulously examined the full lifecycle of coal use (extraction, processing, shipment, burning, ash disposal, etc.) and all the health and environmental impacts created along the way (deforestation, water pollution, air pollution, and disease) in order to identify the real cost of coal-generated electricity.[27] Their findings showed that "accounting for all the [coal-related] damages conservatively doubles to triples the price of electricity from coal." The authors highlighted that this *true* cost makes "wind, solar, and other forms of nonfossil fuel power generation, along with investments in efficiency and electricity conservation methods, economically competitive."

Coming full circle, it is true that everyday levels of CO_2 are not toxic to health. It is also true, however, that many of the products released alongside CO_2 are indeed toxic. Additionally, CO_2 poses a massive, albeit indirect, threat to human health through climate change and all of its associated impacts (extreme weather, sea level rise, food security, drought, etc.). By curbing carbon dioxide emissions, we have an exciting opportunity on our hands. An opportunity to slow global warming and dramatically improve air quality and human health in the process. I say we jump on it!

27

Extreme Weather Is Old News And Is Not Due To Climate Change

While it's true that extreme weather events have always been around, it's also true that they're on the rise. In the United States alone, the frequency and severity of major climate-related natural disasters has risen sharply over recent years. The National Centers for Environmental Information maintains a record of U.S. natural disasters that cost $1 billion or more in damage.[28] On average since 1980, about six such disasters occur each year. In 2016, however, 15 disasters struck. And in 2017, the number climbed again to 16 major disasters. This is nearly three times the average for the recent period. In 2017, the associated costs of these climate-related disasters exceeded $300 billion!

Of course, no single storm can be linked to climate change, just as no single puff of cigarette smoke can be tied to lung cancer. However, we can look at overall patterns between smoking and lung cancer and deduce that the two are related. Furthermore, when toxicologists succeed in identifying specific biological pathways through which smoke can cause cancer, the link becomes even stronger. In the case of climate change, the pathways through which warming leads to more extreme weather are well understood, thus reinforcing the connection between the patterns we've observed with warming and extreme weather. Since it's not necessarily intuitive as to how global warming should make weather more extreme, and even how weather patterns have changed thus far, let's take this section to explore, using just a couple of examples from the recent past.

The International Panel on Climate Change (IPCC) has warned that global warming will produce increased storm severity. Its 2014 Synthesis Report notes that "intense tropical cyclone activity" in the North Atlantic has already taken place and that "extreme precipitation events will become more intense and frequent in many regions."[29] Complimentary findings by a 2006 study from the Massachusetts Institute of Technology states that human activity is "likely responsible for long-term trends in tropical Atlantic warmth and tropical cyclone activity."[30] Sophisticated models consistently agree with the notion of stronger hurricanes. But how in the world are hurricanes and warming connected? To understand this, you need only know that hurricanes are fueled by heat. Therefore, as the climate warms and places like the Caribbean experience record-breaking rises in sea surface temperature, a normal category three or four hurricane can instead become a category four or five.

That hurricanes feed on ocean heat is a principle that is widely understood. As one study notes, "as climate change causes the atmosphere and, in turn, the seas to warm, the ocean stores more energy that is converted to hurricane wind."[31] As for extreme rain events, a warmer ocean means more evaporation and more atmospheric moisture. More moisture of course means more rain. It's therefore unlikely a coincidence that extreme flooding has been on the rise.

Just last fall, we witnessed a dramatic saga unfold in Houston as Hurricane Harvey slammed the Texas coast, dumping more rain than any previously recorded storm in the contiguous U.S. Why was the storm so bad? While several factors likely contributed, there was an important difference between Harvey and its predecessors. Generally, as hurricanes grow, their high-speed winds churn up deeper, cooler water. This cool water calms and slows the storms. In the case of Harvey, deep water was churned up, but the underlying water was warm, not cool. Thus, the calming effect was missing, and the storm retained its power. Adding insult to injury, the magnitude of precipitation allowed Harvey to last longer over land because the immense flooding meant the storm could continue feeding off the energy of its own underlying flood waters, as if still over ocean! This is a departure from your typical hurricane or tropical storm. It's not clear if this is a sign of things to come, but increasing temperatures and warming sea surface waters certainly provide a good reason to pay attention.

As last year's hurricane season wound down in the U.S., an already unprecedented summer of wildfires across the Pacific coast only managed to intensify. In October came the most destructive wildfire in California history, claiming over 5,600 structures and 22 lives.[32] Not two months later, the Thomas Fire became the largest fire on record in the state, scorching over 280,000 acres.[33] In just the last three months of 2017, the state experienced five of its twenty most destructive wildfires. That should cause us some pause. And California hasn't been the only record-breaker. In Oregon, 14 of the 20 largest wildfires on record in the state occurred in just the last two decades.[34] Similar trends have been observed throughout western Canada.

The U.S. National Climatic Data Center shows clearly that average temperatures in California have been steadily increasing since the early 1900s.[35] As drought conditions become more frequent and vegetation drier, the risk of major wildfires is likely to only grow. According to a 2006 study of wildfires in the western U.S., recent decades have seen a four-fold increase in major wildfires, compared to the period from 1970 to 1986.[36] The area burned by such fires has grown a staggering six-fold!

A recent IPPC report confirms expected "decreases in winter precipitation over the southwestern USA" associated with the "expansion of subtropical arid regions." Amidst California's roaring infernos in 2017, California Governor Jerry Brown put two and two together, calling the fires the "new normal."[37] Meanwhile, a 2013 U.S. Forest Service study confirms that "fire potential is expected to increase in the Southwest . . . and Pacific coast, mainly caused by future warming trends."[38] As The connection between wildfires and warming may be somewhat intuitive, but let's take a look at the driving forces nonetheless.

Fire activity is on the rise due to four interrelated factors linked to climate change; namely, earlier snowmelt, higher summer temperatures, a longer fire season, and an increase in vulnerable areas such as high-elevation forests. That is, as global warming produces higher temperatures in the West, snow melts earlier in the season. Snow pack is crucial to feeding creeks and streams and in turn preventing landscapes from drying out during summer. However, as snow melts earlier, vegetation dries sooner, becoming flammable earlier in the season. Coupled with increasing summertime temperatures, this makes for a longer fire season.

Today, the western U.S. experiences a 78 day longer wildfire season than it did decades ago, with the average burn duration having increased from 7.5 to 37.1 days.[36] This is no subtle change. It only exacerbates the problem when we consider that previously inflammable high-elevation regions are now becoming vulnerable to fires as temperatures rise. All told, this sets the stage for a ferocious fire season. While last year's fires were likely made worse by increased vegetation (fuel) following record winter rains the year before, the trend towards increased fire activity for the West is unlikely to be temporary as Earth's temperatures continue to rise.

Beyond hurricanes and wildfires, global warming is also impacting the so-called polar vortex. In Chapter 42, we'll discuss how this is leading to its destabilization and in turn warmer temperatures in the north and colder temperatures further south. Such impacts played out dramatically over the past two winters. Precipitation is also being affected by warming. In this case, the connection is more intuitive. Warmer waters mean more evaporation, and warmer air means more storage capacity of water vapor by the atmosphere. Combining these factors sets the stage for a perfect storm. A perfect *rain* storm, that is, since more water in the air means more water to fall from the sky.

Torrential downpours are resulting in record floods in the U.S. and around the world. In referring to new storm patterns, some are describing "rivers in the sky," waiting to empty at any moment. Hawaii knows this all too well, having made headlines this past April as it incurred more rainfall in a single day than any prior U.S. storm on record. According to the Washington Post, flash flooding and mudslides destroyed roads, bridges, and homes, cutting off locals and leaving thousands of tourists stranded.[39]

Although we've already discussed rising temperature at length elsewhere, it's worth emphasizing that heat records are among those getting broken. This past May 2018, temperatures across the contiguous U.S. were 5.2°F above average, "making it the warmest May in the 124-year record," according to the National Centers for Environmental Information.[40] Temperatures even "surpassed the previous record of 64.7°F set in 1934, during the dust bowl era." Much of Europe similarly sizzled in record breaking heat that month.

Jobs & the Economy

28

Environmental Regulation Is Bad
For The Economy

The notion that we must choose between the economy and the environment is one of the most common misconceptions about environmental issues. It is in fact quite feasible to optimize the two. We can maintain economic prosperity while simultaneously protecting our air, waterways, lands, oceans, and climate. History even tells us so. If we look at the last three decades of the twentieth century, when U.S. environmental law began to seriously grow and take shape, we find the economy was generally thriving. It was thanks to such effective environmental laws that the country managed to avert many environmental catastrophes that may have otherwise ensued, and did ensue in other countries.

Despite such evidence to the contrary, industry often maintains that environmental laws cause undue hardship to production, employment, and ultimately to the economy. In his book *The Making of Environmental Law*, Harvard Law

School professor Richard Lazarus points out that "the actual cost of pollution controls have... almost always proved to be less than those industry projected in initially opposing their imposition."[1] He goes on to highlight several key examples that prove his case. Let's take a look.

In 1990, as Lazarus points out, industry estimated that volatile organic compound controls applied to stationary sources (power plants, factories, etc.) would cost $14.8 billion per year. What was the actual price tag? Around $960 million. Another example comes from 1989, when the utility industry opposed acid rain programs under the Clean Air Act that would limit sulfur dioxide emissions. Industry estimated that such policies would cost between $4.1 and $7.4 billion per year. The estimated cost after the fact? About $1-2 billion per year. Let's turn to the automobile industry.

Strict pollution controls on cars and trucks have never been a favorite to automobile manufacturers, with some calling such emissions reductions "impossible" to achieve. We know from experience that this was a gross exaggeration and that such technology was readily within reach. Thanks to Corporate Average Fuel Economy standards, which forced innovation, fuel efficiency has gone way up over the years, enabling a steady decline in tailpipe emissions and allowing for cleaner air in our cities. Today, you'd be hard pressed to drive two minutes without spotting a hybrid car on the road.

A final example draws from our earlier story of the ozone hole and is perhaps the most interesting of all. When research began uncovering the damaging effects of chlorofluorocarbons (CFCs), the chemical industry quickly moved to the usual defense. A CFC ban would result in "major economic disruption." Meanwhile, as the seriousness of the issue only became more apparent, industry managed to quickly whip up an ozone-safe chemical substitute to replace CFCs, and the economy carried on.

More often than not, evidence refutes the notion that the environment and economy are incompatible with one another. So why does industry make such a fuss over regulations and exaggerate claims of undue hardship? I suspect that two underlying reasons are at play. For one, pollutions controls, while often cheaper than industry predicts, are not cost-free. And just like any *person*, companies would rather not pay an added cost if they can avoid it. In the case of corporations, management is particularly keen on prioritizing profits given their commitments to shareholders. Secondly, companies, like people, don't like change. They would much rather maintain "business as usual" than navigate a whole new system of compliance, not to mention the structural or process changes that come with it.

What is sadly inherent in industry's indiscriminant protection of profits and practices is a disregard for the costs and detriment incurred by society. When a factory pollutes the air, for instance, that pollution affects the health of neighboring communities. But who pays the bill when someone's child is admitted to the hospital with asthma? Certainly not the company. In economics this is called an "externality," or more specifically a negative externality. It's an example of a market failure, in which the cost of something (in this case pollution) is placed on someone else who did not wish to incur that cost. Each year, for instance, air pollution from coal-fired power plants causes somewhere between 10,000 and 20,000 excess deaths in America.[2] Again, these impacts are borne by the public, not the coal companies. Ideally, we would have these external costs internalized, and reflected in the price of coal-generated electricity. In this way, the company would have to account for its more realistic operating costs, and the market could respond accordingly, perhaps choosing other sources of energy if the coal-generated electricity was too expensive.

In the case of climate change, fossil fuel companies have been freely polluting the atmosphere with carbon dioxide for decades. Similarly, sectors such as the agricultural industry have been destroying forests, polluting the water, soil, and air, while accelerating global warming, without having to account for these added costs of operation. As the impacts of climate change exacerbate damages caused by coastal erosion, hurricanes, floods, habitat loss, wildfires, and other disasters, should the multi-billion dollar industries contributing most heavily to the problem really be insulated from the wreckage associated with their products, while the rest of us pick up the tab? Were the government to enact policies to require the internalization of such costs, these polluting industries would need to charge quite a bit more for their products, in turn giving a well-deserved comparative advantage to less polluting competitors. If we truly want a rational and functioning market, then we need to enable informed decisions and adequately account for all costs of production.

29

A Carbon Tax Is Just A Way For The Government To Take Our Money!

This claim neglects the fact that not all taxes are created equal. Scientists agree that carbon emissions need to urgently be reduced. And economists agree that a carbon tax would be the most economically efficient way of achieving this, as opposed to a top-down regulatory approach. Politically, however, advocating for a "tax" is a good way to lose elections. Therefore, few politicians want to touch such proposals. Fortunately, there are creative, revenue-neutral ways of rolling out a carbon tax that would not cost the consumer. By revenue neutral, I mean that tax revenues would not go to the government, but instead to the public. This turns out to be an important piece of many carbon tax proposals that we mustn't overlook.

One well-known iteration of such a plan has been proposed by a nonprofit, nonpartisan, grassroots organization called the Citizens' Climate Lobby (CCL). Called the Carbon Fee & Dividend, their plan essentially places a fee on carbon emissions at the points where fossil fuels enter the U.S. market—at the coal mine, well-head, or port of entry.[3] The revenue generated from this fee would then get equitably redistributed back to the American public as cash. Through this system, carbon-intensive industries essentially get penalized and green industries rewarded. That is, carbon-intensive products get more expensive, which incentivizes consumers to seek greener alternatives. In turn, companies with low "carbon footprints" benefit. Since it's a revenue neutral system, this plan wouldn't increase the size of government or require added regulations, instead making use of market-based incentives.

In 2014, a widely respected firm carried out an economic analysis which estimated that after ten years, a program of this kind would decrease carbon dioxide emissions by a third, increase national employment by 2.1 million jobs, and, for a family of four, return an average monthly dividend of about $300.[4] Over time, as the tax would continue to increase (to further reduce carbon emissions), families would receive an even greater monthly kickback. Once enacted, a plan of this kind would give a whole new meaning to the word "tax"—the kind of tax nobody would want to go away!

A similar population-friendly tax plan called the Carbon Dividend Plan was recently proposed by the Climate Leadership Council (CLC), and authored by leading conservatives James Baker and George Shultz who served as Secretary of State under Presidents George H.W. Bush and Ronald Reagan, respectively.[5] Carbon pricing programs that involve the added step of returning tax revenue directly to the population would likely earn public support, which is one reason they're being supported by Democrats and Republicans alike. Compared to other plans, conservatives in particular like that the CCL and CLC proposals allocate no tax revenue to the government.

If revenue is generated through a tax, but then just given back to everyone, it is reasonable to wonder how exactly this tax achieves anything. How are incentives created, and how do clean industries benefit? Let's take a closer look, using oil as an example. If the government places a tax on the extraction of domestic crude oil because of the carbon dioxide emissions it will generate, we can safely assume that companies will raise the price of oil, and ultimately the cost of gasoline will go up, since gasoline is made from oil. In this way, industry will have passed on the carbon tax to the consumer. Over time, those who drive long distances in gas-guzzlers will have filled up their tanks more often than those who commute on bikes or drive hybrids or economy cars. Having purchased more gas over time, the former group will have felt the carbon tax more than the group who seldom purchases gas. Every month, when the government then cuts an equal-sized check to return revenue to tax payers, that check will more than offset the carbon taxes that "green" commuters paid (since they didn't buy much gas), while falling short of offsetting the taxes that frequent gas consumers paid. In this manner an incentive is realized. Those using fuel efficient modes of transportation saw a financial bonus, while those using fuel-intensive transportation saw a net loss.

The key to the plan is the non-uniform consumption of carbon-intensive products (in our example gas) across the economy, coupled with the uniform redistribution of the related tax revenue, thus creating winners and losers.

Again, the estimated monthly return for a family of four is in the ballpark of a few hundred dollars per month. So in terms of winners and losers, we're probably only talking about differences of tens of dollars. But this adds up and would ideally be sufficient to shift society to less fuel-intensive lifestyles over time!

In terms of industry, the example of fuel prices would spill into many sectors. Let's take the case of fruit sold at the grocery store. Currently, you might not see much of a cost difference between apples shipped from 100 miles away versus apples shipped from 1,000 miles. With a carbon tax affecting the price of gasoline, this difference would be amplified. The apples shipped from further would theoretically cost more. For some consumers, this might be enough to tilt them to the more locally grown apples. While not even knowing it, the consumer just made a "green" purchase! The example here can be applied to all types of commodities and consumer products.

As carbon pricing influences purchasing decisions in society, the market too would adjust, with *green* companies and products being rewarded by increased customers and sales. Fuel-efficient vehicles would likely gain in popularity. And greater incentives would be in place for electricity to be sourced from solar, wind, and other renewables as cities and towns strive to avert the elevated electricity costs associated with coal and natural gas.

As mentioned, the carbon tax plans we've discussed also stipulate a gradual increase in the carbon tax with each year. This increase continues up to a limit, thus amplifying incentives and aiding the transition until a target carbon price is reached. What constitutes an ideal target price for carbon is debatable, and partially depends on the extent of carbon reductions desired. What is not debated is that a gradual year-by-year increase to a specified price target is better than a large overnight shift, as it would ease the economic transition.

To price carbon, the American people would of course have to overcome the kneejerk rejection that comes with that three-letter word "tax." But this seems achievable and begins with awareness. Once onboard, the public can demand Congress to consider such proposals. A bill that offers a path to carbon reductions while stimulating net job growth through the renewable energy and energy efficiency sectors would undoubtedly be popular, and benefit both the nation and world.

30

Green Energy Is Killing Jobs!

R hetoric surrounding climate change as it relates to jobs can be addressed using some simple thought experiments. First, let's consider the notion that renewable, or *green*, energy will somehow kill jobs. If this is true, what jobs would be killed? Well, given the laws of economics, presumably those in competitive industries; coal, nuclear, and natural gas. The nuclear industry doesn't employ many workers except when constructing new power plants. And since nuclear plant construction has mostly been dead for about three decades in the U.S., we can basically forget about any meaningful job support from nuclear. So how about coal? According the Bureau of Labor Statistics, the entire U.S. coal industry currently employs only about 50,000 workers—or as a 2014 article in *The Washington Post* put it, "fewer people than Arby's" (the restaurant chain).[6] That comparison was actually made back when coal employed about 25,000 more people than it does today. Even in America's most coal-productive states, coal still doesn't employ all that many people. Take West Virginia for instance, which is among the nation's leaders in coal production. As of 2010, direct employment by the coal industry on average accounted for less than 5% of total employment in top coal-producing counties throughout the state. Employment by the industry as a whole has only continued to decline in the years since.[7]

How about natural gas-related jobs? Have they been hurt? Absolutely not. In fact, much of the decrease in coal-related employment is directly tied to growth in the natural gas sector—not due to the expanding renewable sector, but rather a fossil fuel competitor! The natural gas industry has seen a dramatic growth over the last decade or so, largely due to technological breakthroughs known as horizontal drilling and fracking, which have enabled the industry to tap into fossil fuel reservoirs that were previously not economically feasible to drill. Such growth has even outpaced that of renewables![8]

According to the U.S. Energy Information Administration, as of 2017 consumption of natural gas had risen nearly every year for the last decade.[9] Meanwhile, U.S. coal consumption continued a decline of nearly 40% since 2005. In 2006, the U.S. consumed more coal than natural gas (in terms of energy-equivalent). By 2016, however, natural gas accounted for twice the energy consumption of coal. The story of declining coal consumption is the same across other developed countries. In the U.K. for instance, coal-fired electricity production accounted for 42% of electricity generation in 2012, dropping to just 7% by 2017.[10] Meanwhile, electricity generation from natural gas grew by nearly 70%, and electricity from renewables grew by 20%.

To recap, very few jobs have been killed in the energy

sector, and for those that *have* been lost, green energy isn't what's been "killing" them. Job loss is concentrated in the coal industry, and is largely due to competition with natural gas. Of course, renewables have also had a role to play. But as a whole, natural gas and renewables have both been extremely good for employment, not bad. Rather than focus on job losses in isolated sectors of the energy industry, we must look at employment trends throughout the energy industry as a whole. This will give us the best indication of what the future of energy means for employment. Fortunately, the outlook is positive!

Key findings from the 2017 U.S. Energy Employment Report show that employment by the energy as well as energy efficiency sectors increased by 300,000 jobs in 2016, accounting for 14% of the nation's job growth.[11] Over the same year, employment grew by over 73,000 jobs in the solar sector, and by nearly 25,000 jobs in the wind sector. Of the 1.9 million workers in electric power generation and fuel, 800,000 contributed to the production of "low-carbon" electricity, which includes renewable energy, nuclear energy and natural gas. Additionally, over 20% of the 6.5 million employees in the U.S. construction industry worked on projects related to energy efficiency. And let's not forget the motor vehicles industry, in which over 250,000 of its 2.4 million jobs were supported by alternative fuels vehicles, a number that increased by 69,000 in 2016 alone. Thus, the minimal job losses we discussed earlier have already been more than compensated for, thanks to growing jobs in the low-carbon energy areas.

What about the globe, you ask? Worldwide, the renewable energy sector employed 9.8 million people in 2016, marking a 1.1% increase from the prior year. Asia in particular is employing an ever-growing number of workers in the renewable sector, now accounting for over 62% of the global total for renewables. According to a 2017 report by the International Renewable Energy Agency, job growth in the solar photovoltaics (solar panels) sector alone rose 12% from 2015 to 2016, employing a total of 3.1 million workers.[12] Similarly, new wind energy installations mostly in the U.S., Germany, India and Brazil contributed to a 7% increase in global wind employment, reaching 1.2 million jobs. Returning to the notion of job loss discussed earlier, these numbers remind us that we can't look at job *loss* without considering job *growth*.

With the innovation and further expansion of natural gas and renewable energy technologies, these sectors are likely to become increasingly competitive. While this is unfortunate for the coal industry, the trend is not likely to reverse, at least not in the United States. Having said that, this is how the economy works. Innovation is always driving out competitors. We should be excited that the renewable sector happens to be a key industry where innovation is rapidly occurring, because it will mean overall reduced carbon intensity as we continue to electrify the world, which will also translate to relatively less greenhouse gas emissions and toxic pollution compared to a no-renewables scenario. And told, renewable energy and energy efficiency projects are growing—not killing—jobs. And their growth is likely to continue. Way to go renewables!

31

The Paris Climate Accord Was A "Bad Deal" For The U.S.

In Chapter 3, I shared my experience at a chili cook-off where I chatted with a nice lady working at a political booth. When asking her about the president's recent decision to withdrawal from the Paris Climate Accord, she replied, "It's too expensive. The U.S. has already given a billion dollars to other countries. We can't afford to give more for climate change." Really? I thought. Ensuring a stable climate for future generations and the survival of our species is "too expensive?" In the president's own words, the agreement was described as a "bad deal" for the U.S. These comments reflect a clear lack of appreciation for the seriousness of the climate predicament that we find ourselves in.

Let's talk about this cost of helping other countries reduce their carbon emissions and the alleged billion-dollar U.S. expenditure. When we hear numbers this large, it's easy to be blown away, since most of us could never dream of having a million dollars, let alone a billion. But we're not talking about you and me here, we're talking about the United States government, which has an entirely different checkbook. $1 billion to our government is a mere rounding error in the nearly $4 trillion annual federal budget. If we spent $10 billion on the Paris Accord, it would still be less than 0.5% of the federal budget—a small price to pay to help avert global catastrophe. And probably a better use of our tax dollars given the future money we'd save by avoiding climate-related disasters.

The frequency and severity of major natural disasters has risen sharply over the years, which means the associated costs to taxpayers (from wreckage) has grown as well. In the U.S., the government maintains a record of U.S. natural disasters costing $1 billion or more in damage.[13] In 2016, $46 billion was spent on such disasters, due to 15 major events. In 2017, major disasters rose to 16, with costs exceeding $300 billion! This shattered the prior U.S. annual record cost of $219 billion that occurred in the wake of Hurricane Katrina and other storms in 2005. In total, 230 natural disasters occurring since 1980 have cost the U.S. over $1.5 trillion. These numbers are critical to take into account when we consider whether paying to reduce greenhouse gas emissions is really a "bad deal." Unfortunately, we don't get to just opt out of global warming costs. We can either pay up front through preventive measures, or we can pay later as more lives are lost, ecosystems are destroyed, and entire communities of people become displaced.

By putting a bit of money towards climate mitigation strategies today, even if it means for other countries, we'll be doing ourselves a service in the long run. We can look at it as an investment! Exercising and eating well may not always be convenient, but it saves a lot in avoided hospital visits and medical costs down the road as we age. Similarly, we need to keep the future of our planet and society in mind, even if it costs a bit more up front.

In his 2009 book *Sustainable Energy without the Hot Air,* physicist David Mackay calculates the amount of money it would cost to shift the United Kingdom completely off fossil fuels by 2050, and then compares this to other grand expenditures.[14] At the time, the U.K. population was about 60 million, compared to 65 million today. According to Mackay's calculation, a major shift from fossil fuels to renewables and/or nuclear would cost the U.K. the equivalent of about $555 billion. This amounts to about $13.5 billion per year. Since really big numbers are hard to conceptualize, let's take a look at some other expenditures for comparison. Again, these are based on Mackay's 2009 figures.

The amount of food waste generated annually in the U.K. totals to nearly $20 billion, while U.K. tobacco tax revenues amount to roughly $15 billion per year. In terms of individual project expenditures, it cost $22 billion to host the London 2012 Olympics, $46 billion to allocate identity cards to everyone in the U.K., $8 billion to build Heathrow Airport Terminal 5, and $15.7 billion for an army barracks redevelopment project. Suddenly, even the most dramatic of renewable energies shifts (100% green energy?) is sounding affordable! Perhaps most relevant for comparison, however, is existing U.K. energy expenditure, which amounts to around $140 billion per year, with an annual market value of consumed energy of about $240 billion. In this context, a $13.5 billion per year investment in renewable energy infrastructure amounts to less than 10% of the country's existing energy expenditure. And again, this assumes a 100% renewable transition for the U.K. Even a 20-30% shift would be terrific and would only amount to 2-3% of existing energy expenditure. As of Mackay's writing, expenditures on renewable energy research and development totaled to only $0.022 billion in the U.K. The prioritization of climate change is clearly missing.

Let's look at some other expenditures to further contextualize Mackay's hypothetical energy transition. In 2008, the U.S. Treasury spent $800 billion on the bail-out of Wall Street banks. The U.K. government spent $925 billion on bailing out British banks. This alone could have paid for the U.K. renewable transition almost two-times over! Moving on, the U.S. spends about $46 billion per year on the "war on drugs," $4.5 billion to maintain a nuclear stockpile, and about $6 billion on military aid in the Middle East. Let's not forget, the recent war in Iraq cost the U.S. over $2 trillion, or about $7,000 per person. Globally, world arms expenditures amount to around $1.2 trillion per year. Given these various points of comparison, the $1 billion that our friend from the chili-cookoff was complaining about now sounds like peanuts—because it is! We haven't even mentioned the $700 billion the U.S. spends each year on foreign oil, or the $40 billion that oil companies like Exxon Mobile make in profits each year.

So what's the global cost of averting "dangerous climate change?" Mackay sites the Stern review, which puts the cost at $440 billion per year, or $440 per year per person if shared equally by the 1 billion richest people. Not too bad to avert global catastrophe! After all, a $2 cup of coffee each day adds up to over $700 per year. In 2005, the U.S.

government alone spent nearly $500 billion on wars and war preparations. That would've been more than enough to cover the tab. If there is a will to address climate change, there is certainly a way. There is a LOT of money moving around the world. We mustn't get disillusioned by the sound of "billions of dollars" and shy away from climate mitigation strategies. It's all about the relative expenditures. The numbers add up, and the funds exist.

32

Pricing Carbon Will Hinder The Free Market

Tax is that three-letter word that just hits the ear all wrong. Nobody likes to see their hard-earned money get chiseled away. It's even more frustrating if you're among the many Americans who believes the government already plays too great a role in our lives. Yet, every day, we pay taxes. We pay taxes when we purchase goods at the store, fill up our gas tank, buy a home, and of course we see a tax deduction on our monthly pay checks. Tax revenues go to all sorts of things. They maintain our courts, police forces, post offices and political institutions as well as keep our roads, water treatment facilities, reservoirs and other infrastructure functioning and up to date.

When it comes to taxes, certain products deemed harmful to society are subjected to an extra tax in order to discourage their consumption and collect some revenue in the process. These so-called "sin taxes" are most commonly placed on alcohol and tobacco products. In recent decades, the world has developed a growing addiction to perhaps the unhealthiest of all products—fossil fuels—and miraculously without a meaningful sin tax for its harmful carbon dioxide emissions. Nearly our entire economy runs on fossil fuels: powering our cars, ships, and airplanes; heating our homes and electrifying our cities—not to mention their use as building blocks for making plastics, chemical inputs, and other synthetics. For all of these perks, we must be grateful, for society has advanced dramatically. Yet, with each pound of fossil fuel we burn, we release more carbon dioxide into the atmosphere, which hangs around for over a hundred years, as well as many toxic pollutants harmful to human health.

Similarly, society has grown accustomed to purchasing all sorts of food products at the grocery store at prices that are disconnected with their true costs of production. In many countries, an aspiration for the Western diet is resulting in an increased consumption of beef and other products known to contribute heavily to global warming through their energy-intensive nature and emissions of greenhouse gases such as methane and nitrous oxide (See Chapter 43). Some researchers who have taken the time to calculate *all* the impacts associated with beef production (deforestation, air pollution, water contamination, etc.) estimate the true cost of a hamburger at about $8!

In the case of fossil fuels, alternative technologies harnessing solar and wind energy are readily available now to assume the primary role in supplying power. Thus, we have arrived at a crossroads in which we must ask ourselves a question: Why are we not using tax incentives to reward the *green* economy and discourage consumption of a harmful fossil fuel-based economy? Similarly, why are certain agricultural products such as beef and dairy priced without consideration for their heavy carbon and other pollutant emissions, which are known to exacerbate global warming, pollute the environment, and harm society? Where are the sin taxes here? These externalized costs represent market failures that are widely recognized by economists. A so-called "carbon tax" is one strategy that would address these externalities (See Chapter 29). This would essentially raise the price of products that emit carbon dioxide into the air, mostly through energy consumption, thus offering a comparative advantage to goods and resources that don't use fossil fuels in their production.

Critics will claim that a carbon tax interferes with the "free market." To this I must point out that we don't live, and never have, in a free-market society. Many foreign products that enter the U.S. are subject to border tariffs in order to give domestic products a comparative cost advantage or at least level the playing field. Domestically, we similarly select winners and losers in the marketplace. How? Through government subsidies. For instance, the U.S. meat and dairy industries have long been subsidized, which has allowed their various products to remain artificially inexpensive. Ever wonder why a veggie burger costs as much as a beef burger, or why many vegetable products at the market are comparable in price to their meat counterparts? Well, the meat industry has received a whopping $10 billion in federal subsidies over the last 22 years.[15] Similarly, dairy subsidies have amounted to about $5 billion. Meanwhile, the most highly subsidized fruit/veggie product (apples) only received $261 million over the same time period. So much for promoting healthy food!

In terms of energy, the fossil fuel industry has also benefitted from exuberant subsidies. Estimates show that fossil fuel subsidies worldwide average between \$400–600 billion annually, compared to only \$66 billion for renewables.[16] This suggests an insufficient willingness to break our addiction. Similarly in the U.S., fossil fuel subsidies between 1950 and 2010 were over seven times higher than for non-hydropower renewables, according to a Washington D.C. based consulting firm.[17] Oil subsidies alone amounted to \$369 billion, compared to just \$81 billion divided between the various non-hydro renewable energy sectors. The effect of this favoritism has had profound implications. In the case of oil, subsidies have served to depress the cost of gasoline and other fuel-intensive products and services in the United States. Sounds great, right? However, let's recall that we live in an age where alternative energy sources exist. Solar, wind, and other renewable technologies can electrify the grid in ways that don't release harmful greenhouse gases. Combined with electric vehicles and adequate charging stations, we can see our way to a low-carbon energy future, with less air pollution and fewer climate impacts. However, these promising technologies can only be so competitive in the face of regulations that continue to favor the heavy polluters.

Even as subsidies to renewables have increased in more recent years, subsidies to the already well-developed fossil fuel industry persist. The Environmental Law Institute noted in its 2009 report that the "substantially larger subsidies to fossil fuels" represent a financial aid to a "mature, developed industry that has enjoyed government support for many years," compared to the "relatively young and developing" renewables industry.[18] From 2002 to 2008, the report found that the fossil fuel industry received about $72 billion in subsidies, "representing a direct cost to taxpayers," compared to $29 billion for renewable fuels. Increasing the amount of government subsidies to the renewable energy industry is an important way we can incentivize green energy entrepreneurs and support the expansion of this sector. Again, if this sounds counter to the notion of a "free market," remember that we're not operating in a free market to begin with.

For those with a steadfast "keep government out" perspective who remain unconvinced of the need for increased renewable energy subsidies, we can still agree on something. A good start to paving the way for renewable energy would be to remove the existing subsidies that are regularly being offered to the already mature and successful fossil fuel industry. Similarly, we should consider reducing subsidies to the mature and highly polluting meat and dairy industries. These steps would do more to keep the government out of the marketplace, while simultaneously taking us where we need to go in terms of reduced carbon pollution. And it's consistent with free market economics. Let's make it happen!

Conflicting Evidence

33

CO_2 Levels Aren't Really Increasing

This happens to be one of the easier claims to debunk, since we have direct carbon dioxide measurements that have been collected by various university and scientific organizations for decades. The most well-known data documenting the growth in global carbon dioxide levels comes from Charles David Keeling. As a postdoctoral researcher at the California Institute of Technology, Keeling chose to dedicate his work to measuring carbon dioxide in the atmosphere. Many had written this off as a silly idea, since CO_2 was regarded as a stable gas in the atmosphere; that is, it neither increased nor decreased much from year to year. However, Keeling thought otherwise.

Interested in collecting air samples that could best reflect the "global" air, Keeling quickly realized he'd need to get out of the urban environment, far from vehicle traffic and factories, since these are direct sources of CO_2 that were throwing off his early measurements. Thus, he set camp among the nearby secluded and gorgeous redwood forests of Big Sur. However, he still could not get unbiased background measurements. As it turned out, the forests too gave erratic measurements since plants "breathe" carbon dioxide. If you recall from science class, animals inhale oxygen and exhale CO_2, while plants do the opposite! This produced daily fluctuations in Keeling's air samples. Finally, an ideal sampling location was identified. Keeling would travel to the Big Island of Hawaii, establishing his research 10,000 feet up on the shoulder of the active Mauna Loa volcano. Not a bad office! In the middle of the Pacific Ocean, Keeling would be far from major pollution sources. And high above the town and forests, the influences of vegetation and human activity would also be minimal.

For years, Keeling went to work, collecting atmospheric CO_2 measurements each day. While some colleagues would continue to lack the vision of his mission, what Keeling ultimately discovered would serve as a wake-up call to much the world. Carbon dioxide was rising, and it was rising fast! When his measurements on the Big Island began in 1958, the average CO_2 concentration was about 315 parts per million (ppm). Ten years later, that number would reach about 325 ppm. Fortunately, Keeling's research didn't end there. Like a true scientist, his curiosity persisted, and Keeling continued to lead a CO_2 monitoring program atop Mauna Loa until his passing in 2005. The so-called Scripps CO_2 Program at Mauna Loa continues to this day, now carried on by his son Ralph Keeling, a professor of geochemistry at the Scripps Institution of Oceanography in San Diego, California.

Over the life of the Scripps CO_2 Program, carbon dioxide has continued to increase, with each year showing higher average levels than the previous year. Keeling's work showing this steep increase in concentrations dating back to the 1950s resulted in a depiction (graph) of CO_2 that has famously come to be known as the "Keeling Curve," shown in the schematic in Figure 5..

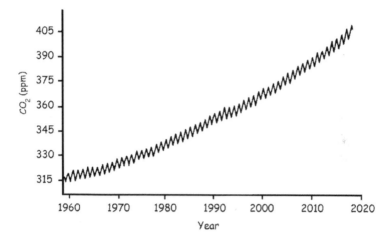

Figure 5. Schematic of the Keeling Curve, showing a steep and steady rise in CO_2 levels over time, as well as seasonal fluctuations.

You'll notice in Figure 5 that CO_2 levels rise with a bit of a sawtooth pattern. This is because atmospheric CO_2 fluctuates with the seasons. A minor drop occurs during spring in the northern hemisphere while an increase occurs in fall. This is because plants shed their leaves in the fall, which releases carbon back to the atmosphere, whereas the opposite occurs in spring as plants blossom and take in new carbon from the air. Since most of Earth's land mass resides in the north, the opposite pattern in the south is not enough to offset this effect. Therefore, seasons in the northern hemisphere drive this sawtooth pattern. This seasonal rise and fall of CO_2 based on plant activity is often referred to as

Earth "taking a breath." In fact, forests are known as the "lungs" of the Earth for the same reason.

We can thank Keeling for his committed work in consistently documenting changes in atmospheric CO_2. His research sounded an early alarm that called international attention to the potential of an impending climate crisis. Unfortunately, the world did not take immediate action and still has made only minimal progress in addressing the issue. However, it's not too late to arrest the worst climate impacts to come. It begins with awareness—hence this book—and then action!

Climate skeptics will sometimes suggest that because Keeling's measurements were collected atop a volcano, the CO_2 data must be skewed by volcanic emissions. Keeling wasn't measuring "global" carbon dioxide, they'll assert, but rather volcanic activity. No wonder his measurements were high, right? Not so fast! First, it's not that his measurements were "high," it's that they increased year after year. This is what made them important. Of course, volcanic emissions wouldn't be increasing with each passing year unless the volcano was gradually "waking up," which isn't the case. More importantly, however, Keeling and his team were well aware of the influence of volcanic CO_2 from Mauna Lau. Most of the time, however, the prevailing winds carried volcanic emissions in the opposite direction of the observatory, presenting no issue. When the winds occasionally reversed, sometimes in the early hours of the morning, the volcano's influence was very obvious and could be taken into account, so as not to skew the data. That is, Keeling and his team were careful to exclude volcanic CO_2 measurements, so as not to bias the data away from reflecting background CO_2 levels.

What's also important to note is that Keeling, while famously calling early attention to rising CO_2 levels, has not been the only one measuring the gas. Shortly after his initial findings, research around the world began to confirm his measurements, with a network of CO_2 monitoring stations by Keeling's team and others being ultimately established from the North Pole to the South Pole. If you visit the NASA website, you can even view CO_2 measurements in real-time. The Scripps CO_2 Program website will let you do the same. Each year, CO_2 levels continue to rise, consistent with the trajectory observed by Keeling.

34

What About Mid-Century Cooling?

While global temperatures have been rising sharply for over a century, there was an interesting departure from this uphill trend that took place between about 1940 and 1975. During this period, temperatures appeared to stabilize, and even cool a bit. The cooling was only slight—about 0.2°F—but it was cooling nonetheless, and it took place while greenhouse gas emissions were still going up and up. So, what happened? The explanation is fascinating, and ironically has to do with the same culprit responsible for CO_2 emissions and global warming—namely, fossil fuel burning.

The greatest source of carbon dioxide emissions from human activity comes from the burning of fossil fuels. During the cool period in question, particularly in the post-WWII period, the industrial economies of the United States and Europe were soaring to new highs. With rapid industrial expansion came massive increases in energy use, which meant more fossil fuel combustion and more air pollution. Use of coal and oil were particularly on the rise. Coal is the dirtiest of the fossil fuel "three amigos," followed by oil, and then natural gas. Dirtier fossil fuels contain more chemical impurities (meaning more harmful air pollution) and release more carbon dioxide per unit of energy produced when burned (meaning more global warming potential). One of the most important air pollutants released when burning coal and oil is sulfur.

Sulfur emissions are problematic for several reasons. Not only does sulfur harm human health and cause acid rain, destroying crops and property in the process, but it also plays a role in climate change. When burned, sulfur is released to the atmosphere as sulfur dioxide. These gaseous molecules ultimately react in the atmosphere to form microscopic particles called sulfate aerosols. These aerosols are important to our story because they reflect sunlight. That is, they basically do the opposite of what greenhouse gases do. Interestingly, volcanoes also emit sulfur and have been documented to influence global temperatures (by reflecting sunlight) following major eruptions (See Chapter 3). Wow, you say, we can just release a bunch of sulfate aerosols to fix the climate problem! Some are indeed proposing this, but we'll save that discussion for Chapter 45. Now back to our story of mid-century cooling!

As the U.S. and Europe ramped up their coal and oil use, levels of sulfur in the atmosphere began to rise dramatically. This meant a substantial increase in the ability of the atmosphere to reflect incoming sunlight. It is unlikely that the increased capacity of atmospheric reflection and sudden trend towards global cooling were mere coincidences. Rather, the abundance of light-reflecting aerosols is believed to have played a role, counteracting the warming effects of greenhouse gases that had been accumulating, and in turn pausing the trend of rising temperatures. So why didn't this last? Why did cooling cease in the mid-1970s, suddenly giving way to more prolonged warming? Hasn't our fossil fuel use only continued to rise? If so, it would seem more sulfate aerosols would rise too, thus perpetuating the cooling effect. So what happened? The explanation ironically has to do with environmental policies to control air pollution.

In the U.S., the 1970s were kicked off by landmark environmental regulations, such as the 1970 National Environmental Policy Act, the Clean Water Act of 1972, and the Ocean Dumping Act, as well as the establishment of the U.S. Environmental Protection Agency (EPA) to create and preside over such rules. The first official Earth Day even commenced on April 22, 1970. All of this translated to a major shift towards reduced environmental pollution of all sorts. It was a *green* start to the decade! Thanks to the Clean Air Act of 1970, air pollution began to curtail sharply as well, saving an estimated 200,000 premature deaths in its first 20 years of existence. One of the main air pollutants we curtailed was sulfur pollution. While this meant great things for our health, it was also a rude awakening to the greenhouse gas problem brewing beneath the surface. By cleaning up the air and reducing sulfur, we essentially removed the thin reflective mirror we had created, which had been masking us from global warming for several decades.

Wait a minute, why didn't sulfur hang around? After all, we'd been pumping heavy amounts into the atmosphere for many years. In the case of greenhouse gases, we're often told that stopping emissions today would still mean warming for decades to come, thanks to the stubborn "already released" gases that would continue to hand around. So, what's the story with sulfur? Where is the long-term cooling effect? As it turns out, sulfur is not the type of chemical to linger for long in the atmosphere.

The lifetimes, or "residence times," of CO_2 and sulfate aerosols in the air are quite different. Sulfate only lasts days to weeks before naturally dissipating, whereas CO_2 can float around for a hundred years or more. This means that the cooling effect of sulfur emissions is very short-lived while the warming effect of carbon dioxide is long lasting. An exception is when powerful volcanoes inject aerosols high into the stable stratosphere, in which case they can remain for a year or more. While the continuous pumping of sulfur into the air during the mid-century may have allowed sulfur to partially offset the effects of CO_2, producing slight cooling, the flighty nature of sulfur meant that its compensatory effect was only temporary. In the end, the gradual accumulation of long-lived CO_2 and other greenhouse gases would win, becoming the main driver of the modern climate.

Despite some slight cooling of air temperatures around mid-century, evidence suggests that Earth as a whole was still warming during this time period. In addition to looking at average air temperature, insight about temperature trends can be seen in daytime maximum and nighttime minimum temperatures. During the mid-century period, average maximum daytime temperatures declined. This is consistent with the overall temperature decline we've discussed, and makes sense given the light-reflecting capabilities of sulfate aerosols. However, at night there is no sunlight, and therefore nothing for sulfur to reflect. What happens to temperatures after dark can therefore better indicate the temperature trajectory of the planet in the absence of aerosol influence. So, what did the data show? Temperatures were rising—particularly in the 1950s. That is, minimum nighttime temperatures were going up because the accumulation of greenhouse gases were preventing less and less heat from escaping back to outer space at night, suggesting the greenhouse effect was indeed becoming more pronounced. Aerosols were depressing temperatures during the day, but the warning signs for a heating planet were present after dark.

35

Paleoclimate Records Show That Co₂ Rises After Temperature Rises—Not Before!

Although we can demonstrate experimentally that carbon dioxide indeed traps heat, leading to warmer air temperatures, it's also useful to look at the paleoclimate record. The "paleoclimate" refers to the entirety of Earth's climatic history, or at least as far back as science will let us look. Believe it or not, scientists can use isotopic ratios taken from deep ice cores, ocean sediments, and other ancient substances to understand Earth's temperature dating back millions of years (See Chapter 2). Quite impressive, right? Scientists can also reconstruct a similarly long CO_2 record. Given that carbon dioxide is a greenhouse gas that traps heat, you might suspect that temperature and CO_2 levels would go hand-in-hand throughout Earth's history. When one goes up, the other goes up, and *vice versa*. As it turns out, that's exactly what we see! Well, sort of. Let's discuss.

Projecting temperature and CO_2 levels over the past several million years indeed shows a strong correlation between the two. Given what we know about the warming effects of CO_2, this is not a shocker. What is *more* interesting is that in many cases temperature appears to rise first, followed later by CO_2. Climate skeptics will point this out as evidence against carbon dioxide as a cause of global warming. How can we blame carbon dioxide for global warming if the warming precedes the CO_2? It's a fair question. But let's not give up before exploring the answer.

The first thing to note is that Earth's paleoclimate record is mixed. In some cases, changes in CO_2 predate changes in temperature. In other cases, the opposite is true. Given what we know about the warming effects of CO_2, one can easily make sense of the first scenario (more CO_2 leads to warmer temperatures). But what about the reverse scenario? How can we make sense of temperatures rising *before* CO_2? To answer this, it's important to understand that Earth is a dynamic system. Things do not occur in isolation from one another, and in fact many phenomena play off one another in a so-called "feedback" process (See Climate Change 101). The interplay between temperature and CO_2 represents an important case of positive feedback, in which increases in either CO_2 or temperature can trigger increases in the other. While we already know how CO_2 causes temperatures to rise, let's use an example to understand the reverse scenario.

As temperatures go up, frozen areas such as the tundra begin to thaw. This thawing means that microorganisms can go to work breaking down organic matter in the soil. These biodegradative processes release carbon dioxide and methane into the atmosphere. Since both are powerful greenhouses gases, their release "fuels the fire" for even greater warming. Essentially, a snowball effect has kicked in. Frighteningly, this is exactly what's taking place in the tundra today. Now back to the paleoclimate.

Let's envision another scenario in which temperature causes CO_2 to increase. It may come as a surprise, but much of the carbon dioxide we emit into the air does not stay there. Where does it go, you ask? Into the land and oceans. Carbon dioxide dissolves into water to become carbonic acid. This makes the oceans more acidic, which turns out to have ecological implications which we just discussed in Chapter 25. However, we should thank the ocean for its carbon-absorption, because without it we'd be in a whole lot more trouble. Atmospheric CO_2 levels would be much higher, making the climate that much warmer. The flip side to having carbon stored in the oceans is that it can get rereleased back into the atmosphere if the waters warm up. This is not unique to the oceans, but is a physical trait of water and other liquids in general.

Warm water holds less dissolved gas than cool water. Therefore, heating water will cause the release of stored gas. In the case of the ocean, a warmer ocean means the release of CO_2, again kickstarting a positive feedback loop. More CO_2 means more warming, which means greater CO_2 released from the oceans and even more warming, and so on. There are other examples of how temperature rises can produce rises in carbon dioxide, but you get the point. The important takeaway is that it doesn't matter whether changes in temperature initiate changes in CO_2, or whether changes in CO_2 initiate changes in temperature. Once the ball gets rolling by either variable, temperature and CO_2

then play off one another, constantly amplifying changes in the other. And it's not just in the warming direction. If for instance the climate were to cool, the oceans would have an increased capacity to absorb and store more CO_2. Less atmospheric CO_2 would then mean less greenhouse warming, and hence even greater cooling.

At this point, you're probably wondering what the initial X factor is that tips either CO_2 or temperature in one direction or another. That is, what gets the ball rolling? The answer is, a multitude of things. It depends on which time period in history you're talking about. The most consistent factors that have initiated temperature changes in Earth's past are collectively called the Milankovitch cycles, which are the planetary cycles we discussed in Chapter 4. Depending on the relative orientation of Earth in terms of its orbit, wobble, and tilt, the planet receives different amounts of energy from the sun, which produces either warming or cooling that varies over tens of thousands of years. For instance, as Earth becomes less tilted, the polar regions experience warmer winters and cooler summers, which favors the growth of ice sheets at the poles. Additionally, when Earth's wobble and orbit are such that Earth is nearest the sun in January (currently the case), growth of the northern polar ice cap is favored.

Recall from Climate Change 101 that ice sheets act as positive feedbacks by reflecting sunlight. When they shrink, they amplify warming. And when they grow, they amplify cooling. This means that when the Milankovitch cycles begin to influence temperatures on Earth, those changes can be readily enhanced, and temperature changes can become dramatic. In past instances, it's therefore reasonable that temperatures would have changed first, followed by CO_2.

Other things that can get the ball rolling include episodic events such as volcanic eruptions and variations in solar activity. As discussed in Chapter 3, a single volcanic eruption can release enough atmospheric sulfate aerosol to cause short term cooling on Earth, while long term volcanic activity can sometimes result in accumulated carbon dioxide and cause warming. In the instance of gradual volcanism over time, increased CO_2 could expectedly precede rising temperatures—as is thought to have been the case when Earth was rescued from its snowball state some 700 million years ago. A meteor colliding with Earth is yet another example of an event with climate-altering potential, as we know from the extinction of the dinosaurs. Similarly, the so-called Little Ice Age, which lasted from about the 1500s to the 1800s was thought to have originated in part from a decrease in sunspot activity known as the Maunder Minimum (See Chapter 41).

Another factor that has proven capable of initiating climatic change on Earth is the "human" factor. Mostly from burning massive amounts of fossil fuels, humans over the last 200 years have released enough carbon dioxide to have increased atmospheric CO_2 by 45%. The magnitude of this increase is on the scale of catastrophic events of our geologic past. Except, the *human* event is perhaps more dramatic given the rapidity with which we've brought about these changes. By now, you know how the story goes. With increased CO_2 comes an increase in—drum roll—temperature! And to no surprise, that's exactly what we're observing today. CO_2 is going up, and temperature is following right behind. Our emissions of other major greenhouse gases such as methane and nitrous oxide, which are even more heat-trapping than CO_2, are only contributing to the warming. And as we know, with a rise in greenhouse gas levels, positive feedbacks such as melting ice sheets and warming oceans also start kicking in, amplifying the warming further.

Interestingly, Earth was, and still should be, entering a period of natural cooling according to its Milankovitch cycles. Our axial tilt is straightening out, and the northern hemisphere winter currently occurs when Earth is closest to the sun. That is, global temperatures should be continuing down. Yet, human activity has released enough greenhouse gas into the atmosphere to completely reverse the trend. Frighteningly, it has taken only 200 years for human greenhouse gas emissions to offset the entire last 6,000 years of cooling that had been taking place! We know from the paleo climate record that temperature and CO_2 don't move perfectly in sync. One usually lags behind the other. In the present case, CO_2 is leading the charge, with temperature hot on its tail. This suggests that we've committed ourselves to a certain amount of warming in the future, even if we decide to halt carbon emissions today. How high temperature will go as CO_2 levels continue to skyrocket is any climate modelers best estimate. We are quite literally conducting a global experiment the likes of which our species has never encountered. One thing is for sure, if we want to limit future warming and halt the experiment, actions to limit further greenhouse gas emissions are urgently needed.

36

Glaciers Aren't Melting,
Antarctica Is Even Gaining Ice!

In 2014, NASA published an article on its website titled, "Antarctic Sea Ice Reaches New Record Maximum."[1] Pretty crazy right? Amidst a warming globe, the South Pole indeed showed gradual increases in sea ice cover for most of the last four decades. How could this happen? Does it refute the notion of global warming? First, recall from Chapter 42 that global warming doesn't mean that warming will be uniform across the globe. The inner workings of the climate are extremely complex, and while we know that global temperatures will rise as we pump more CO_2 into the air, it's much more difficult to predict how each region will respond to such change. As global warming disrupts traditional storm activity, precipitation, ocean currents, and wind patterns, some places are indeed becoming cooler and even gaining ice. Nonetheless, the phenomenon in the south admittedly puzzled scientists. After all, the poles should be impacted the most as the planet warms. So, what has been going on?

Importantly, increased sea ice in the Antarctic does not refute the notion of global warming. Warming around the planet is indeed occurring and is well documented by air and ocean temperatures, irrespective of how individual regions such as the Antarctic respond. Additionally, while sea ice in the South Pole saw decades of growth, sea ice in the Arctic has been in sharp decline for decades, more than compensating for any gains in the south. As a whole, the planet has seen a net loss, not gain, of sea ice. Or as a more recent NASA publication phrased its title, "Sea ice increases in Antarctica do not make up for the accelerated Arctic sea ice loss."[2] The article noted that "As a whole, the planet has been shedding sea ice at an average annual rate of 13,500 square miles (35,000 square kilometers) since 1979, the equivalent of losing an area of sea ice larger than the state of Maryland every year."

Okay, so the planet is warming, and global sea ice has been decreasing. This still doesn't explain why the Antarctic showed increases in sea ice through most of recent history. Scientists have worked extensively to figure this out, and their findings can essentially be boiled down to a few likely causes. One explanation relates to melting of Antarctic land ice. As warmer ocean waters cause melting at the edges of the land mass, fresh water is liberated to the sea. Freshwater is less dense, or more buoyant, than saltwater, meaning it floats on top of ocean water. Even when ocean waters are slightly warmer (warmer liquids tend to float), freshwater can nonetheless remain on top because of its lower salinity and density (low density liquids also tend to float). Freshwater also freezes more readily than saltwater. You can see where I'm going here! An abundance of buoyant freshwater at temperatures barely above freezing (since it just melted) flowing into the ocean could foreseeably refreeze and lead to a growth in sea ice.

Another explanation has to do with wind patterns. Cyclonic winds that sit over the South Pole play a big role in the formation of sea ice. When such winds strengthen, sea ice separates, exposing new underlying ocean water to frigid air, enabling it to freeze—thus leading to increased ice coverage. Similarly, when these winds shift directions, the thin ice can get pushed around exposing new underlying water to freezing conditions. Scientists have indeed observed stronger-than-normal pressure systems which have increased winds over certain areas of the South Pole. Thus, this could help explain the pattern of increased sea ice.

Let's turn to the potential role of precipitation. A warming globe means more precipitation due of course to increased evaporation and water storage capacity of the atmosphere. This trend is being observed in areas of the Antarctic as well, where certain regions are experiencing above average snowfall. What this means for sea ice is quite interesting. As snow accumulates on floating sea ice, it can actually push the thin ice below the water, allowing cold ocean water to seep up and essentially flood the snow. This creates a slushy mixture that freezes in the cold air, in turn adding thickness to the ice. This new, thicker ice is more resilient to melting.

Ocean currents may also have played a role. As the planet warms and wind patterns change, underlying ocean currents are also affected. Changes in water circulation patterns may be bringing colder waters up to the surface around the Antarctic landmass, fostering the growth of more ice. The release of freshwater from melting ice—adding buoyancy to surface waters—only further complicates the situation, potentially altering underlying currents in a different way. It's possible that buoyant meltwater has prevented cold surface waters from mixing with underlying waters, allowing the surface to become cooler than normal. Typically, water sinks as it cools and becomes denser, making it difficult for surface waters to freeze. However, with buoyant freshwater on top of denser saltwater, sinking may not occur, allowing surface waters to become colder and colder, and ultimately freeze.

Of the various hypotheses described, no single explanation has gained universal consensus as *the* reason Antarctic sea ice showed decades of gradual growth. It's perhaps a combination of all factors. Importantly, however, the gradual increase of Antarctic sea ice that we've been discussing represents a trend that spanned the period from 1979 to 2015. You'll notice this does not encompass the most recent few years. That's because after 2015, the decades of *gradual* growth in Antarctic sea ice cover gave way to a dramatic shift in the opposite direction. And I *do* mean dramatic! In just two years, January sea ice cover in the southern hemisphere dropped by 45% relative to its 2015 peak.[3] As a NASA article put it, "Antarctica hit its lowest extent ever recorded by satellites at the end of summer in the Southern Hemisphere, a surprising turn of events after decades of moderate sea ice expansion."[4]

As it turns out, the 2017 winter came with record lows for sea ice in both the Arctic *and* Antarctic. However, such a record in the North Pole is consistent with the story of Arctic melting that we've been seeing for decades. It's the drop in the Antarctic which represents something new—a departure from the norm, and a major one at that. Changes in southern hemisphere sea ice coverage typically vary by 10% or 20% over two-year periods. The 45% drop from 2015 to 2017 was therefore unprecedented. Perhaps things have reached a critical mass down south. While 2018 showed a rebound, it was only slight, with wintertime sea ice still at 40% of its 2015 coverage.

Before we conclude, let's touch on the role of sea ice in terms of the climate system. Importantly, sea ice does not play a direct role in sea level rise. That's because sea ice is already floating in the sea, so it has already displaced its share of ocean water. So when we talk about Antarctic sea ice growing, we're not talking about sea levels dropping, somehow offering a counterweight to the melting of glaciers elsewhere. Similarly, as sea ice declines, oceans levels do not rise. So long as ice is floating in the sea, melting that ice or growing that ice won't affect sea levels. It's only when *land* ice retreats or grows, or the oceans warm or cool (thermal expansion or contraction) that sea levels change.

So, what exactly *is* the role of sea ice in terms of the climate? Solar reflection! As we discussed in the last chapter, when more sea ice exists, Earth can reflect more of the sun's radiation. It would be great if the many decades of increased Antarctic sea ice were enough to offset the increased greenhouse effect we've created through air pollution. However, as we've seen, global sea ice has been shrinking, not growing. Therefore, the change in sea ice as a whole has meant a net loss for the globe. And now the Antarctic has even taken a turn. Thus, the future does not look bright for polar ice. In Climate Change 101 we discussed "tipping points." The sudden and dramatic disappearance of sea ice that we just witnessed in the south bears a frightening resemblance to what we might expect should we manage to cross such a dangerous threshold.

37

What About The Warming "Hiatus" A Few Years Back?

Throughout the latter half of the 20th century, global average temperature has increased rather steadily. However, just as the climate issue was heating up (pun intended!) around the first decade of the new millennium, something interesting happened. In its Fifth Assessment Report, the Intergovernmental Panel on Climate Change (IPCC) reported an apparent pause in surface warming from 1998 to 2012, suggesting the rate of global warming had slowed—at least for the time being.[5] Climate skeptics not surprisingly jumped on this so-called "hiatus" as evidence against global warming. Never mind that skeptics should choose to trust IPCC when their data shows a *pause* in global warming, yet deem them liars when their data says the opposite (most of the time!). So what was the "hiatus" all about, and does it really undermine the notion of a warming planet?

First, and importantly, a decade-long pause in

temperatures does not refute the notion of global warming or call into question its existence. Temperature fluctuations and short-term pauses can be expected. They've occurred before and will occur again. In the case of climate change, greenhouse gases still trap heat and are rapidly increasing in the atmosphere. These fundamentals remain unchanged, even if temperatures wiggled around for a decade. Having said that, let's discuss why the recent wiggle took place.

Explaining the "hiatus" requires us to turn to 1998. This marked an extremely warm El Niño event. If you look at the global temperature record, temperatures rose precipitously that year, creating an outlier from the continuous warming trend. By comparison, the relatively lower temperatures of the next few years (when temperatures resumed) gave the appearance of reduced temperatures—a sudden "hiatus" in the warming trend. In actuality, this was largely an illusion thanks to an exceptionally warm El Niño. The outlier that was El Niño was influential, but still not the only reason for the apparent "hiatus."

In its report, IPCC noted that the rate of recent surface warming (during the "hiatus") was smaller than the rate of warming over the prior 30 to 60 years. This statement stirred up a lot of skeptic energy. However, a problem with this comparison, which IPCC even acknowledged, is that the recent trend was a bit too short to tell us much. In other words, it's not fair to compare a robust long-term trend with a short 14-year window. The latter is simply not enough time to allow a meaningful trend analysis. It might give us some interesting insights, but it must be interpreted with caution. Had just another year or two gone by, a record-warm 2014 would have been enough to influence the trend.

Hiatus or not, the temperature trend that took place over the first decade of the twenty-first century has now given way to an extremely sharp temperature rise. According to NASA, 17 of the 18 warmest years in our 136-year record have all occurred since 2001.[6] The exception was 1998 (that El Niño year!). Such statistics make disputes over the old "hiatus" sort of a moot point.

38

Sea Levels Around Greenland Are Falling!

The notion of sea levels falling around Greenland is actually no myth and needs no correction. However, the take-home message from this observation is often misconstrued. So let's set the record straight. The expectation from warming seas and melting glaciers is that oceans will rise globally. At least, this is what *reason* tells us. So what's up with Greenland? Let's ask Harvard University geophysicist Jerry Mitrovica, who mapped out the changes in sea level that could be expected from the collapse of the Greenland ice sheet. As it turns out, predicting regional sea level rise from the melting of Greenland requires an understanding of Greenland's gravitational pull. For those who don't know, Greenland is an enormous island that sits to the northeast of Canada. Despite its name, Greenland is actually covered in snow and ice. Literally, there's almost nothing green about Greenland! The island has been cold and accumulating snow for so long that its ice sheet stands over a mile thick in some places. That's a HUGE chunk of ice!

Believe it or not, the ice on Greenland is so large that it even has its own gravitational pull. Although this sounds mind blowing, Greenland is actually not unique in this regard. All bodies of mass exert *some* gravitational force. For most objects, the force is negligible. In the case of the moon, its mass is so large as to influence our ocean tides, even at nearly 240,000 miles away! But you don't have to be the moon to affect sea levels. What Greenland lacks in size it makes up for in proximity to the ocean. Greenland's gravitational pull on its surrounding ocean has effectively created a bulge of higher water around its surrounding seas. Other coastlines exhibit influential gravitational pulls on their surrounding waters as well. However, most land masses aren't piled a mile-high in ice, and therefore aren't going anywhere (won't affect sea level) as temperatures rise.

What has made Greenland a spectacle in recent years is an apparent drop in its surrounding sea level. Climate skeptics say that "melting glaciers" and "sea level rise" don't add up. That is, if Greenland ice is melting, shouldn't its surrounding sea levels be increasing? Well now you know there is more to the story—a gravitational component! As Greenland melts, it's mass shrinks, thus exerting less of a gravitational pull on surrounding waters. As it turns out, the "reach" of Greenland's gravitational pull is quite large, expanding 1,200 miles out from its coast. Should the Greenland ice sheet collapse entirely, this would mean that places as far away as Norway and Sweden could experience drops of sea level on the order of meters, according to Mitrovica.[7] Meanwhile, sea levels elsewhere in the world would rise substantially, particularly in the southern hemisphere.

In addition to the gravitational pull that comes with Greenland's tremendous mass, the mile-thick ice is also exerting immense pressure on the underlying Earth. As it turns out, Earth's crust is not totally resistant to this weight. Just as the weight of your body produces a footprint as you walk across the dirt, the weight of Greenland's ice similarly causes a depression in the Earth. As ice on the island melts, this weight lessens, and the underlying Earth actually begins to rebound upward. This "post-glacial rebound," as it's called, is yet another important reason why sea levels around Greenland are dropping.[8] Although, in this case we're not seeing a true drop in sea levels, but rather upward moving earth. The land is literally rising from the water! A recent study shows uplifts of nearly half an inch per year (12 mm) in certain areas of Greenland.[9]

Between 1979 and 2006, summer melt on the Greenland ice sheet grew by 30%, reaching a new record in 2007.[10] This has translated to a LOT of water added to the world's oceans, and a lot of mass being lost from this particular point on the globe. In recent decades, melting has only accelerated. A Danish research collaborative monitoring Greenland and Arctic ice notes that, since 2002 alone, Greenland has lost over 3.6 trillion metric tons of ice.[11] Should the rate of melting continue uninterrupted, scientists project continuous major ice loss, and thus an increase in global average sea level. Knowing what we do about the gravitational pull and the weight of ice, however, this global average increase can be expected to come with drops in sea levels around some areas. This does not refute global warming but is in fact consistent with expectation once we take other important factors into account.

39

Greenland Used To Be Green,
So The Earth Must Be Cooling.

It's a bit odd that an island mostly covered with ice should be called Greenland. Intuitively, one might assume the island was named once upon a time when the land was sprawling with forests and grasslands. Were this true, it would suggest that the climate must have since cooled, leading to the accumulation of enough snow and ice to bring it to its present form. However, Greenland received its name around the year 982 A.D. For the island to have transitioned from warm and green to a land buried a mile high in ice over just a thousand years, centuries of some pretty extreme cold and snow would have needed to occur. This would reasonably seem at odds with the notion of a warming planet, right? So what's the deal?

Before we dive in, it's tempting to point out that neighboring Iceland, which would intuitively be ice-covered, is actually beautiful and green (even a popular tourist destination!). Science aside, this alone sort of cancels out the logic that an *ice* land named Greenland serves as evidence for recent cooling, since we have a *green* land named Iceland that sits next door. That is, if Greenland's ice proves recent cooling, shouldn't Iceland's lack of ice prove recent warming? So, which is it? Did the area cool or did it warm? After all, the two islands were named around the same time and are located not far from one another. As it turns out, we shouldn't infer too much from the names of Greenland and Iceland—at least, not about the past climate. Let's take a closer look.

We know from ice core measurements that the Greenland ice sheet is at least 100,000 years old. That is, it didn't suddenly appear over the last millennium. So, there goes the notion of a "once green" Greenland! Why, then, the unusual name? As it turns out, Greenland and Iceland were both named by Viking explorers around the end of the first millennium A.D. According to a recent National Geographic article on the topic, it was Norse tradition around that time to name newly discovered lands based on the sights that first met the eye.[12] For instance, when Vikings initially set foot on present-day Canada, the land was named Vinland, or "Vineland," because of what looked to be grapes growing near the shoreline. Similarly, legend has it that Iceland was named by a Viking who climbed atop one of its mountains, only to discover a fjord full of icebergs.[13]

In the case of Greenland, its naming followed a less traditional path. The island's first permanent European resident was well-known Viking explorer Eric the Red, who settled the island after being exiled from Iceland. Eric is said to have named the island Greenland in the hopes that it would attract more settlers. While Greenland only boasts a population of about 56,000 people today, the slogan at the time was allegedly successful in drawing new colonists to the island.

Although Greenland's name wasn't inspired by lush countryside, it's nonetheless believed that Greenland was warmer at the time of its early settlement than it is today—just not warm enough to make much difference in ice cover. This period of warmth, from about 950 to 1250 A.D., is known as the Medieval Optimum, or Medieval Warming Period, and appears to have been most pronounced in the North Atlantic, including southern Greenland.[14] Such warming eased ocean travel in the region. It's likely no coincidence that Viking exploration and settlement was successful throughout this period. Ultimately the prolonged warmth would end, and colder summers and encroaching sea ice would eventually descend on Greenland, threatening crops and ultimately forcing the colonies to abandon the island. For more on the Medieval Warming Period, and its underlying causes, turn to the next chapter.

40

What about the Medieval Warming Period?

We saw in the last chapter that most of Greenland was cold and ice-covered, even in 982 A.D. when it earned its name by a Viking explorer. Nonetheless, temperature reconstructions using ice core and ocean sediment data do suggest the period was probably warmer at the time than in the centuries before and after. This period from 950 to 1250 A.D., known as the Medieval Warming Period, has led some to assume that present-day warming must therefore be natural and harmless. Temperatures were up a thousand years ago, life seemed pleasant, and now they're up again. No big deal, right? As you're probably guessing, it's not that simple.

First, warming during the Medieval Warming Period does not appear to have been global, but rather regional, isolated mostly to the North Atlantic and a few other areas. This is in stark contrast to the "global" warming we're experiencing today. Also, to the notion of natural warming, the temperature rise during the medieval period was indeed natural. Since data from a thousand years ago is of course limited, we cannot be certain as to what caused the warming. However, sunspot records suggest that increased energy from the sun likely played a role. Some scientists also point to reduced volcanic activity. Because we weren't there, and data from the past is limited, we'll likely never fully know all the factors that played into medieval warming. Fortunately for us, those same data limitations do not apply today. And as we've discussed, recent warming correlates well with recent increases in greenhouse gas levels.

It's tempting to find comfort in the Medieval Warming Period since temperatures were similar to those of today and life seemed just fine. However, there are key differences we must keep in mind. As noted earlier, medieval warming does not appear to have been global. Also, temperatures today are continuing to rise. The planet is currently about 1.3°F (0.7°C) warmer than it was in the mid-1900s, and the medieval climate was perhaps 0.9°F (0.5°C) warmer compared to the same period. By the year 2100, however, global average temperatures are projected to increase by somewhere between 3-7°F, or about 1.7-4°C, relative to pre-industrial times. This blows both last centuries warming and medieval warming out of the water! In the United States, annual average temperatures over the next three decades alone are forecasted to rise by at least another 2.3°F (1.3°C) relative to the recent 1976–2005 period.[15]

As a final note, the climate in some cases has fluctuated somewhat regularly over shorter time scales. As University of Chicago geophysicist David Archer points out, there is a "hint of a 1500-year cycle in climate" over certain glacial periods, including our own interglacial period.[16] Some might therefore argue that the Medieval Warming Period and Little Ice Age (See next chapter) were pieces of such regularity, and that today's warming is similarly just part of the cycle. However, as Archer notes, the 1500-year cycles of recent times only show up in a specific area of the world, again suggesting a regional—not global—cycle. If by any chance the Medieval Warming Period and Little Ice Age were part of some regular cycle that scientists had yet to figure out, it could indeed mean we are in for natural warming over the next few centuries. But as Archer notes, "The existence of a 1500-year cycle would not make the forecast of global warming wrong." Human activity is still releasing potent greenhouses gases that are trapping heat and warming the planet. Instead, "The 1500-year cycle would make the forecast worse." We'd get the effects of natural warming *plus* human-caused greenhouse warming.

41

We're Just Emerging From
The Little Ice Age

From about 1500 to 1800 A.D. temperatures were cooler than they are today. In Europe, where the cooling was most pronounced, average temperatures were up to 1°C lower than modern levels. In addition to being cooler, the climate during this so-called "Little Ice Age" period was characterized by rather erratic behavior compared to the climates either prior or after. Decades of cold were followed by decades of drought, then warmth, then extreme rain, and so on. Finally, after centuries of a cooler climate, warming began to return, ultimately bringing us to where we are today.

The Little Ice Age reinforces the idea that climate change is natural. One century it's warm and a couple of centuries later it's cold. And rightfully so, because many natural phenomena do indeed influence the climate from one century or millennium to the next. However, when the climate changes it is not due to some law of nature that says it's time to change, or because it suddenly decides to. In the case of the Little Ice Age, Earth did not spontaneously emerge from the cold period. Rather, key shifts took place in certain climate forcing factors (See Chapter 23) that caused the climate to change.

Scientists have a good idea of at least one major factor that likely caused and ultimately ended the Little Ice Age. Similar to the Medieval Warming Period, it has to do with solar activity, or more specifically sunspots. Recall from Climate Change 101 that sunspots are dark spots on the gaseous surface of the sun. When sunspot activity is high, Earth receives increased energy from the sun. And similarly, when there are few sunspots, less radiation shines down on the planet. As it turns out, the Little Ice Age coincides with a period of very few sunspots, known as the Maunder Minimum, named after English astronomer Edward Walter Maunder. While technology to detect various phenomena was of course limited several centuries ago, records of sunspot activity were nonetheless possible. Very large sunspots can sometimes be seen with the naked eye at sunrise or sunset when the sun is most dim. However, no records of naked-eye sunspot sightings exist during this cool period from about 1645 to 1715. Scientists using the newly invented telescope to observe the sun at the time similarly observed few sunspots.

Also coinciding with the Little Ice Age were two other major periods of reduced sunspot activity, occurring just before and after the Maunder Minimum.[17] The Spörer Minimum, named after German astronomer Gustav Spörer, took place from 1460 to 1550, while the Dalton Minimum, named after the famous English meteorologist, physicist, and chemist John Dalton, occurred at the tail end of the cold period (1790-1830). These spans of record-low sunspot activity would have meant reduced solar energy reaching Earth at the time. Cooling during the Little Ice Age therefore makes sense. With that said, the Little Ice Age was not a *true* ice age. It was a period of extended cooling that primarily affected the northern hemisphere. With a slightly dimmer sun shining down over the entire Earth, one might wonder why temperatures dropped so substantially and why such changes were only regional. That is, why didn't the entire globe cool? The answer probably has to do with ozone and jet stream winds in the upper atmosphere.

Recall from Chapter 13 that the ozone layer exists in a stable region of the upper atmosphere known as the stratosphere. This protective layer forms as high-energy ultraviolet light interacts with oxygen molecules. With reduced solar activity during the Maunder Minimum, less ozone would have formed. According to NASA scientists, reduced ozone in the stratosphere would have changed jet stream wind patterns so as to shift the so-called North Atlantic Oscillation (NAO) into a negative phase. When this pressure balance is negative, winter storms traveling over the Atlantic tend to head eastward for Europe, creating a more severe winter for the region. In contrast, a positive phase NAO means winter storms travel north, and Europe experiences milder conditions. Results using advanced computer models confirm that the influence of reduced solar energy during the Maunder Minimum would have resulted in a negative NAO, and thus cooling over Europe.

Another possible contributor to the Little Ice Age has to do with something known as the "thermohaline circulation." Often called the "conveyor belt," this important ocean circulation brings warm equatorial water to the North Atlantic via the Gulf Stream current. It's in fact thanks to this transport of warm water that much of Europe gets to enjoy temperate weather, despite sharing the same latitude as frigid Siberia. Key to the movement of this warm current is an area near southern Greenland where the current becomes dense and sinks, ultimately banking off the ocean floor and returning south. During the Medieval Warming Period, scientists believe that massive water runoff from nearby glacial lakes may have dumped enough freshwater into the North Atlantic to prevent the conveyer belt from sinking (since fresh water is less dense and floats)—thus disrupting the northbound flow of warm water and casting Europe into a cool period. A "shutdown" of this conveyor belt also helps to explain why cooling during the Little Ice Age was regional, as opposed to global.

When comparing the Medieval Warming Period with today, some draw a frightening parallel. That is, the rapid melting of Greenland, like the glacial runoff before the Little Ice Age, could suffice to once again dilute the North Atlantic, shutdown the conveyer belt, and plunge Europe into another cool period. Although interesting, an important difference today is the dramatic rise in global temperatures that has accompanied greenhouse gas emissions. Thus, the prospect of an impending mini ice age for Europe is likely overblown.

42

Some Areas Are Getting Colder, So Where's The Global Warming?

All too often, people cite cold weather as evidence refuting the notion of global warming. First, recall from Chapter 21 that there's an important distinction between *weather* and *climate*. That is, *climate* refers to long term (30 year) weather trends, not day-to-day or even year-to-year variability. Second, we must recognize that global warming refers to an increase in the average temperature of the planet as determined by monitoring stations around the entire world. Given that we're talking about an *average*, it's not unreasonable that some places would experience cooling under a global warming scenario. So long as cooling trends are outweighed by warming, then we still have global warming. This possible confusion is why some scientists prefer the term "climate change," which better accounts for the fact that the climate is not warming everywhere. Let's look at a recent example of a counterintuitive temperature extreme to help us understand the complexity of the climate and how even cold temperatures fit into the picture of global "warming."

For a recent example of record cooling, we need look no further than our neighbors in the Northeast. As noted in Chapter 44, Boston just broke a near-hundred-year cold record last December. So, what's going on? To understand, we must know that record cold in the Northeast did not happen in isolation. Rather, record cold in the area was met by record warmth in other areas. The two anomalies were related. That is, while December delivered record lows to Boston, Alaska was bathing in record warmth.[18] Scientists attribute this unusual weather to the instability of the so-called polar vortex.

As the name suggests, polar vortices are circulating wind patterns that sit over Earth's poles. When they are strong, frigid temperatures remain relatively isolated to the polar regions. However, recent warming trends have weakened these winds. In the north, the vortex has consequently begun to meander more on its otherwise circular path around the pole. This meandering motion has allowed frigid Arctic air to dip further south over certain regions, while warmer equatorial air penetrates further north.

Jason Box, who is a professor in glaciology at the Geological Survey of Denmark and Greenland, ascribed the recent temperature abnormalities across the northern U.S. and Arctic to greenhouse warming "enhanced by human burning of fossil fuels."[19] He described the Arctic as "warming at twice the rate of areas to the south" and called the instability of the polar vortex a "signature of climate change."

Importantly, weather around the world breaks records in all directions all the time. Recalling that *weather* is not *climate*, we've got to be careful not to cite any one weather event as evidence for or against climate change. Instead, we need to look at long-term trends. Despite record-breaking cold in Boston last winter, an underlying trend of warming is still evident. A comparison of daily record high temperatures with record low temperatures averaged across the U.S. for instance, shows a trend of increasing record highs over the years. According to the National Center for Atmospheric Research, the current ratio of record high to record low temperatures is about 2:1, with climate models suggesting this could increase to 20:1 by mid-century.[20] This indicates a trend consistent with the notion of global warming and the buildup of heat-trapping CO_2.

Probably the most notorious example of someone misunderstanding the meaning of global warming and the complexity of the climate is the snowball that was thrown by Oklahoma Senator James Inhofe while on the Senate floor in February of 2015. The senator had fetched a snowball from outside as proof against global warming. He was clearly unaware of the distinction between weather and climate, and the regional implications of climate change. Ironically, Inhofe happened to be Chairman of the Senate Committee on Environment and Public Works at the time. *Some* chairman!

The Flip Side

43

More CO$_2$ Is Good For Plants And Agriculture!

As you might recall from science class, animals breathe oxygen and plants breathe carbon dioxide. Having said that, you might suspect that more CO$_2$ in the air would lead to healthier plants. You wouldn't be entirely wrong, as experiments do confirm this. So, does this mean all the CO$_2$ we've been spewing into the atmosphere is a good thing, fostering healthier forests and productive agriculture? Not so fast! Things are far more complex. First, there is a saturation effect that limits the plant growth we can expect from adding more and more CO$_2$ into the air. That is, the more carbon dioxide goes up, the lower the benefit. This is somewhat intuitive if you simply think about oxygen and humans. Increasing oxygen might improve some physiological processes at first, but pumping more and more oxygen into your lungs won't turn you into Superman!

A second and very important point is that this so-called "CO$_2$ fertilization" effect cannot be looked at in isolation.

Touting carbon dioxide's benefits to photosynthesis without describing its downsides of increased heat stress and dryness is a bit like bragging about the healthy salad you ate for lunch without mentioning the French fries and scoop of ice cream that came on the side. We can't cherry-pick the healthy sides of our diet and expect to understand our personal health. Similarly, if we're to comprehend the full impact that rising carbon dioxide will have on plants, we must consider its impacts to temperature, soil moisture, precipitation patterns, and other key factors that are also tied to plant health.

For decades, scientists have studied the complex role that CO_2 plays in plant physiology. If you isolate a plant in a laboratory and increase CO_2, you'll indeed observe more photosynthesis and growth. However, the world is much more complex than a laboratory. For instance, some key crops, like corn and sugar cane, are already efficient at absorbing carbon such that adding more CO_2 doesn't do much. Even more importantly, plant growth is not solely governed by CO_2 intake. Just as animals need oxygen AND food, plants need CO_2 AND other nutrients. In a recent interview with *Scientific American*, environmental research fellow Richard Norby of the Climate Change Science Institute of Oak Ridge National Laboratory points out that "*nitrogen* is often in short enough supply that it's the primary controller of how much biomass [plant mass] is produced."[1] He goes on to say that "if nitrogen is limited, the benefit of the CO_2 increase is limited... You can't just look at CO_2, because the overall context really matters." In the U.S., soils are well fertilized such that nitrogen limitation isn't a major issue. However, the same cannot be said for Africa and other parts of the world.

Other important factors that keep plants happy include water and mild temperatures. As we know, CO_2 emissions are heating the planet and impacting the distribution of precipitation and river flow. Frances Moore, an assistant professor of environmental science and policy at the University of California, Davis, notes that "Even with the benefit of CO_2 fertilization, when you start getting up to 1 to 2 degrees of warming, you see negative effects."[1] This results from "soil moisture deficit [or] heat directly damaging the plants and interfering with their reproductive process." Moore also notes that increased CO_2 benefits weeds as well, which compete with farm plants.

In many areas, CO_2-driven climate change is leading to desertification that is literally transforming landscapes. In southern California, where I live, temperatures have risen more than other states, leading to droughts and record-breaking wildfires, which are only projected to worsen.[2] Much of Australia is in the same boat. University of Melbourne researchers comparing Australian droughts over the last 400 years found the recent Millennium Drought of 1997–2009 to be "very much below average" in terms of both its extent and duration.[3] The executive director for the Water Services Association of Australia was quoted at the time as saying "We are trying to avoid the term 'drought' and saying this is the new reality."[4] Fortunately for agriculture, more CO_2 happens to increase plant water efficiency. That's because when CO_2 is more abundant, plants can afford to shrink their microscopic carbon-intake holes (called stomata), and thus reduce evaporative water loss. While this will undoubtedly help plants cope with heat stress and droughts in the future, it'll be insufficient to prevent net crop losses in many cases.

In a 2016 NASA study that considered changes in CO_2 as well as CO_2-related climatic impacts, findings using a series of global models showed that a doubling of atmospheric CO_2 would lead to mixed results for different crops.[5] Wheat and soybeans crops were projected to fare the best, with the positives fully outweighing the negatives. Wheat yields in particular were shown to increase by 8-10%. Results for corn on the other hand were not so good. Corn would suffer 8-15% losses in yield, largely because its existing efficiency at using CO_2 means it wouldn't gain enough from added CO_2 to offset the negative impacts of higher temperatures and drier conditions. For rice, the CO_2 positives would compensate for most of the negatives, but overall we could expect a slight loss. In terms of natural ecosystems, experimental evidence suggests that, while more CO_2 increases plant productivity, such effects aren't permanent if soil nutrients are low.[6]

Although CO_2 buildup is leading to warmer temperatures and heat stress around the world, certain regions are experiencing more, not less, rainfall. While this sounds great, this can mean torrential and erratic downpours that damage crops. A field of corn can't reap the benefits of a rainstorm when it arrives as a sudden downpour that sweeps the field away—as is happening in India and parts of the U.S. According to the 2014 National Climate Assessment, "Rainfall's erosive power is expected to increase as a result of increases in rainfall amount in northern portions of the United States."[7] Even in places like Iowa which haven't seen increases in total annual precipitation, the report notes there has nonetheless been "a large increase in the number of days with heavy rainfall." It goes on to say, "By mid-century, when...precipitation extremes are further intensified, yields of major U.S. crops and farm profits are expected to decline." How does sunlight play into all this? The report states that a "Reduction in solar radiation...due to increased clouds and humidity...is projected to continue and may partially offset the acceleration of plant growth [from higher CO_2]."

In addition to its erosive effects, rainfall, if too sporadic, can be of little benefit to crops. Rain falling on a dried-up field of dead wheat, for instance, doesn't do anyone any good. California knows this all too well. As described in the 2014 report, climate change will lead to "an increase in both the number of consecutive dry days...and the number of hot nights." Not to mention, "chilling requirements for fruit and nut trees in California will not be met by the middle to the end of this century." All told, plenty of evidence suggests that crop yields will be negatively, not positively, affected by increased CO_2—that is, after we account for the full list of CO_2-related impacts. Let's turn now to crop-related impacts to nutrition.

Higher CO_2 levels tend to alter crops' nutritional content—and not for the better. As Samuel Myers, principal environmental health scientist at Harvard University, puts it, "We know unequivocally that when you grow food at elevated CO_2 levels in fields, it becomes less nutritious."[1] Why does more CO_2 and rapid growth mean less nutrients? The report cited earlier explains that since "soil may not be able to supply nutrients at required rates for faster growing plants, plants may be smaller, reducing grain, forage, fruit, or fiber production." Myers also describes losses of "significant amounts of iron and zinc," as well as protein. As CO_2 levels rise, some scientists are concerned that nutrient losses in food products could be sufficient to cause protein and zinc deficiencies in an estimated 150 million people by mid-century.[1] This is on top of rampant deficiencies that already exist around the world!

A point worth making in our discussion of CO_2 and crop yields is the often-overlooked fact that much of the food we grow never even gets eaten. In the U.S. for instance, it is a sad reality that about 30—40% of the food we grow winds up in the dumpster.[8] That's over 200 pounds of food per person each year! This takes into account the food wasted at restaurants (when people don't ask for a to-go box), damaged in transport, dumped by grocery stores after expiration dates (expiration dates don't actually mean much!), not purchased by grocery stores because of being oddly shaped (two-tipped carrots, double-chinned potatoes, etc.), as well as the food that spoils in household cabinets and refrigerators. When combined, annual food waste is staggering. Returning to our discussion, it begs the question of whether we have a food *productivity* problem or a food *waste* problem. Agricultural productivity would go a lot further if we'd simply eat more of the food we produce. That is, we don't need CO_2 fertilization, we need food conservation!

As it relates to climate change, food waste is of even greater concern when one considers the enormous role the agricultural sector plays in contributing to climate change. Growing food requires an immense amount of water, fertilizer, land area, and usually pesticides. Each of these has energy and carbon associated with it. For instance, in developed nations water is not just water. It must first go through a water treatment plant, which uses energy and in turn releases carbon dioxide (since most energy is produced by burning fossil fuels). The water then gets pumped to farms for irrigation, which again requires energy. Pesticides and fertilizers also require fossil fuels— as actual ingredients and as energy sources for processing and transport. And let's not forget deforestation. Agriculture requires land, which often means chopping trees through slash-and-burn methods. This results in the direct release of CO_2 and the removal of an important carbon sink, since plants absorb CO_2. We haven't even talked about the fuel and energy used in post-harvest processing and shipment. All of this adds up. Thus, the agricultural industry has an immense "carbon footprint," accounting for about 20-30% of the total greenhouse gases that human activities release each year.[9] This is no small piece of the pie! In general, animal products, particularly beef and dairy, require far more energy to produce than plant products and therefore have the largest carbon footprints on a calorie-for-calorie basis.

In addition to impacts through greenhouse gas emissions, the agricultural sector is responsible for a great deal of other pollution. When rains fall, pesticide and fertilizer chemicals don't stay put, but instead get carried away with water runoff, polluting neighboring rivers, lakes, streams, and ultimately the ocean. Considering that livestock alone accounts for 30% of Earth's land surface, this adds up to a LOT of water pollution.[10] This sector also releases the lion's share of human-related ammonia emissions, thus contributing to acid rain and the acidification of ecosystems (See Chapter 13).

The fact that we waste so much food as a society means that we waste far more energy, deforest far more land, and release far more pollution and greenhouse gas emissions than we need to. And food waste is not merely an American problem. In the European Union, food waste amounts to about 20%, most of which occurs at the household level.[11] Even developing countries waste food, albeit mostly at the level of storage, transport, and processing—such as when poorly maintained roads cause shipment delays that lead to food spoilage. By the way, let's not forget that food is *food*, and that many countries face hunger issues. Even in the U.S., an estimated one in six Americans lack a secure supply of food.[12] By reducing food waste just 15% in America, we'd be able to feed over 25 million more people each year.[8]

Recall how this chapter began, discussing the prospect of higher CO_2 levels boosting plant growth and crop yields. Although we saw that a full accounting of CO_2-related impacts (not just the added CO_2 itself) would increase yields for only certain select crops, it has hopefully become clear that even this small benefit to food production pales in comparison to the colossal food waste problem we have today, particularly in the U.S. If we want benefits related to agriculture and food products, we must address food waste. And while this chapter mostly discussed the pros and cons of CO_2 in the context of plants and agriculture, we mustn't forget broader impacts. That is, the "benefits" of CO_2 fertilization do not occur in isolation. They occur with a laundry list of adverse impacts that more than offset the positives, such as sea level rise, desertification, extreme flooding, coastal erosion, heatwaves, wildfires, climate refugees, species loss, and—let's not forget—reduced yields for certain types of crops and regions.

44

Who Cares About 2 Degrees C Of Warming?

Since 1970, the average surface temperature on Earth has increased by about 0.3°F (0.17°C) per decade.[13] While this is over twice as fast as the long-term average dating back to our first available direct measurements (1880), this admittedly doesn't sound all that extreme. Depending on our greenhouse gas emissions, global average temperatures are likely to increase at least another couple of degrees by the end of the century.[14] With that said, 2°C of warming relative to pre-industrial temperatures is the "dangerous" level we're often told we mustn't cross if we're to avoid global catastrophe. In Fahrenheit, this corresponds to 3.6 degrees of warming. But again, what's the big deal? Who cares about a few degrees of extra heat when temperatures in a single day can fluctuate by as much as 10 times that amount? The key is the word "global." A 2°C increase in global temperatures does not mean a mere 2 degree increase in your backyard.

Warming on Earth is not occurring uniformly. Some

regions are getting WAY warmer, while others are getting only slightly warmer. And some places are even getting cooler. In other words, the 2°C increase is an average of all these ups and downs across the world. While on average the temperatures are going *slightly* up, the regional changes are far from slight. And these changes are greatest over land, compared to the ocean.

Even in areas such as the U.S. where *annual* temperatures sound mild, *seasonal* temperatures have become quite extreme. Just this year, Oklahoma hit almost 100°F in the dead of winter.[15] In other states such as Chicago, St. Louis, Philadelphia, and Cincinnati, heat waves have taken record numbers of lives in recent years. In fact, over the last three decades, extreme heat has been the leading weather-related cause of death in the U.S.[16] Heat-related mortality might not sound like a big deal if you're in your 30s or 40s, but if you're among the elderly, a heatwave can mean the difference between life and death. As global temperatures continue upwards, major spikes in regional heat and related fatalities can be expected to rise.

If you live at the North Pole, temperatures are a whopping 11°F (6°C) warmer compared to the 1981-2010 average for the area.[17] Just this February, temperatures at the North Pole soared above freezing despite the region still being enshrouded in total winter darkness—setting a new February heat record according to the Danish Meteorological Institute.[18] By comparison, February temperatures normally average about -27°F (-33°C) for the North Pole. Only months prior, temperatures in Fairbanks, Alaska similarly averaged 20°F above normal.[19] Having the poles bear the brunt of global warming might sound lucky, since fewer people live there to feel the heat. But it's not that simple. This brings us to another major impact of a "slightly" warmer planet; namely, the melting of glaciers and sea ice. Reduced ice coverage means less reflection of sunlight by Earth's surface as well as rising sea levels (for glaciers).

While the planet, as of 2017, has warmed by "only" 1.8 degrees Fahrenheit (1°C) since the late nineteenth century, double-digit increases in northern temperatures are causing massive ice sheets to melt.[20] In his book *Eaarth*, Bill McKibben points out that in 2007 there was 40% less sea ice in the Arctic compared to 1968 when astronauts of the Apollo 8 mission first gazed back at Earth from outer space.[21] This trend has only continued. According to NASA, the maximum sea ice extent in 2018 was 448,000 square miles (1.16 million km^2) below the 1981-2010 average annual maximum.[22] This loss corresponds with an area larger than the size of Texas and California combined! In 2008, both the Northwest and Northeast Passage—usually frozen over—opened as ice-free shipping lanes for the first time in human history. In *Eaarth*, McKibben spells the title with an extra "a" to emphasize that we're irreversibly pushing our planet into a transition from the comfortable Earth we've all come to know and adapted to, into a *new* planet—planet Eaarth—that is unfamiliar and extreme. He makes a sound point worthy of our attention.

In terms of sea level rise, the melting of the Arctic is not a contributing factor. This is because ice in the North Pole is sea ice, which is already floating and displacing ocean water (just as ice cubes in a glass of water don't cause the glass to overflow when they melt). This, however, doesn't mean vanishing Arctic sea ice is not significant. Indirectly, loss of sea ice has consequences for both sea level and all other climate impacts. This is due to positive feedback, as discussed in Climate Change 101. That is, less ice means less reflected sunlight. And when less sunlight is reflected, Earth retains more heat and becomes warmer, thus contributing to even more Arctic melting, and so on. This loop continues. As the melting of the Arctic reinforces this feedback system, temperatures go up and up, causing more melting in not just the Artic but Greenland and other frozen regions of the world. In these ice-covered *land* regions, melting indeed contributes to sea level rise. In this way, the thawing of Arctic sea ice indeed plays a role in sea level rise—just not the direct role that land ice plays.

Let's take Greenland as an example. Unlike in the Arctic, the Greenland ice sheet sits atop land. Melting of this ice therefore has quick and direct consequences to sea level rise. Covered with ice over a mile thick in places, if Greenland ice was to completely melt it would release enough water to raise sea levels by about 20 feet (6 meters). As recent decades have shown, its thawing has already begun. In fact, like the Arctic, Greenland has been a major site of accelerated melting, as shown by the over 3.6 trillion metric tons of ice that have been lost since 2002.[23]

Despite global "warming" trends, the U.S. has not been without its fair share of anomalous blizzards and wintertime chaos. This past winter, the eastern states braced for nor'easter storm after nor'easter. In one case, a "bomb cyclone" packed enough energy to topple power lines, leading to blackouts from Virginia to Maine. Only months prior, the region experienced record cold. In Boston, for instance, the maximum daily temperature in December reached a new low of 12 °F, breaking the city's prior record of 18 degrees set in 1924.

According to the U.S. Global Change Research Program, the Northeast has experienced increased extreme precipitation, with an over 70% rise in the amount of precipitation falling in "very heavy" weather events from 1958 to 2010.[24] Of the 10 heaviest snowstorms in Boston, five occurred since 2000—with two taking place within the same two weeks of 2015, making it the all-time snowiest season for the city. Living in nearby Cambridge at the time, I can recall cross-country skiers taking to Massachusetts Avenue in the wake of the storms. Not your everyday sight!

Consistent with the erratic nature of climate change, perhaps better called climate "weirding," the Northeast received an evanescent surprise of summer-like 70 degree weather right in the heart of its otherwise frigid winter— breaking February heat records for the second year in a row.[25] In 2017, 19 areas across the Northeast experienced their warmest February on record, including Washington D.C., Philadelphia, Buffalo, and Baltimore. Daily temperatures that month broke records dating back to 1906.

While New England is known for its unpredictable weather, recent up-and-down temperature extremes have been uncharacteristic. Scientists attribute this unusual weather to the instability of the so-called polar vortex, which is allowing Arctic air to descend further to the south (See Chapter 42). As an interesting climatic side note, this past winter also marked the first tornado to ever touch down in February in Massachusetts since official records began in 1950. Climate "weirding" again comes to mind.

As weather events across the world break all types of records, an underlying pattern of warming nonetheless emerges. Recall from Chapter 42 that the National Center for Atmospheric Research compared daily record high temperatures with record low temperatures and found a trend toward increasing record highs over time. The ratio of record high to record low temperatures was about 2:1, with projections of a 20:1 ratio by mid-century.

What we've discussed in this chapter is just the tip of the iceberg in terms of the impacts that a 2 degree shift in global average temperature can mean to various regions and climatic systems of the world. A full discussion of impacts would take up an entire book, rather than a chapter. Suffice it to say that the global average temperature is just that, an average. There are a lot of extremes in between. In the case of today's global warming, extremes on the *hot* end are becoming sufficiently abundant and long-lasting to pull the global average temperature upward, despite some colder temperature records that have also been broken.

45

Geoengineering Will Save Us!

Recall from Chapter 3 that volcanic eruptions release something called sulfate aerosols into the atmosphere, which have the effect of blocking sunlight and cooling the Earth. The same aerosols are released when we burn coal and oil, and have in fact been implicated as a contributing factor for the cooling observed during the mid-twentieth century. "Geoengineering" is an idea that essentially leverages this same concept. It refers to the idea of spraying reflective sulfate aerosols into the upper atmosphere in order to reduce the amount of sunlight reaching Earth's surface, and hence prevent the planet from continuing on an uninterrupted path of dangerous warming. In short, geoengineering is a strategy to combat climate change.

Before we dive into some of the pros and cons of geoengineering, bear in mind that geoengineering as of now is only a proposal. That is, geoengineering is not currently taking place. In fact, most governments, including the U.S., have been reluctant to even provide funding to research geoengineering. Some people have taken notice of so-called contrails in the atmosphere, which appear as thin white streaks left behind by airplanes. Importantly, however, this is not geoengineering, but rather the result of internal combustion engines releasing water vapor into cold and/or humid skies, causing condensation—as your car exhaust pipe does on cold, wet mornings, or after it rains.

If contrails are only condensation, why do some planes produce them, while others do not? And why do they appear on some days and not on others? The answer is that no two flight paths are alike, and the atmosphere isn't uniform in terms of its temperature and humidity. Planes flying at some altitudes may therefore fly through areas favorable to condensation, while others pass through warm or dry areas that absorb the vapor trail completely. This is also why some days show many contrails while others show none. On some days the atmosphere is simply more humid, or cooler, than on others. It's true that contrails can lead to cloud growth and in turn influence local weather. However, this is a *byproduct* of air traffic, not the *purpose* of it. Now back to geoengineering!

Geoengineering to avert catastrophic global warming would entail the continuous release of sulfate aerosols into the upper reaches of the stratosphere. Why the stratosphere? Because this is a stable region of the atmosphere where aerosols can be expected to stick around for a while and have the longest effect. Additionally, we'd prefer to keep sulfate out of the lower atmosphere for reasons that have to do with acid rain and air quality (See Chapter 13). So, what about the pros and cons?

Let's begin with the drawbacks. When considering the

prospect of transporting millions of tons of sulfur into the atmosphere, I am immediately taken back to my college atmospheric chemistry course in which my professor used to say, "More pollution is never less pollution." The comment may be more fitting for situations where we dump chemicals into the ocean to clean up oil spills, but the essence of the phrase is that we must be cautious about introducing new chemicals into the environment in the name of "fixing" the environment. Reducing the cause of pollution is always a better bet than trying to slap a band aide on the problem.

In the case of climate change, reducing greenhouse gas emissions is absolutely essential if we are to mitigate catastrophic impacts. Similarly, adaptation strategies are needed to cope now and in the future as the climate changes. While geoengineering projects would not by definition preclude us from taking steps to implement these measures, one can imagine a situation in which geoengineering takes the pressure off, and these much-needed steps become smaller or less immediate.

In effect, geoengineering could become a crutch that enables inaction by government and industry to mitigate and prepare for climate change. Were this to happen, it would mean a dangerous predicament in which temperatures would perhaps stabilize while business-as-usual carbon pollution continues. The effect could be a buildup of climate forcing greenhouse gases without anyone taking notice. If for some reason geoengineering projects were to suddenly come to a halt, say from war or economic depression, we would have effectively unleashed a greenhouse bomb marked by a potentially rapid reversion to original warming. By "rapid" I mean that in a matter of a few years global temperatures could race up in a sort of catch-up game to the levels they would have originally reached had aerosols never been in the equation— somewhat akin to the warming that occurred in the 1970s after we began to reduce sulfur pollution from burning fossil fuels (See Chapter 34). In this regard, geoengineering is a bit like "numbing the pain." It's okay as long as it doesn't prevent us from taking care of the injury!

While not insurmountable, this is certainly a risk that comes with geoengineering. If governments are serious, the issue can be dealt with through stringent policies that commit nations to pre-determined emissions goals. However, we all know that international climate agreements don't always go as hoped, and governments don't always stick to their commitments—take a look at the Kyoto Protocol as an example.

As a pollution scientist, there's another aspect of geoengineering that is very worrisome. That is, what about the unknowns that could arise from what would amount to major polluting of the stratosphere? If you're familiar with the history of environmental contamination, you know that the past is replete with examples of "benign" products or ideas that turned out not to be so benign in the end. A perfect example is the manufacturing of CFCs discussed in Chapter 13. Other examples range from the rampant use of DDT insecticides and PCBs in the 1960s—ultimately banned in the 1970s—to endocrine disrupting BpA that was commonly used in plastics until very recently. Geoengineering proposals may sound more straight forward. But the atmosphere is a complex place and involves complex chemistry and physics. We should therefore be careful in tampering with it.

Releasing enough sulfur to meaningfully reduce sunlight would presumably mean releasing enough sulfur to cause other problems should we fail to understand the full implications of geoengineering. It's also worth noting that sulfur aerosols, once sprayed, would not remain in the stratosphere indefinitely, but would dissipate after about a year or two. This means that geoengineering would not be a onetime shot. It would instead require constant replenishing of aerosols. This means not only increased costs, but potentially increased consequences if things don't work out as planned. Not to mention, where is all the sulfur going as it dissipates? This is where issues of pollution again come in.

A key impediment to the notion that "geoengineering will save us" deals less with geoengineering itself than the ethics and politics involved in the question of "who owns the sky?" I don't mean literally. Nations of course have their own designated air spaces. But rather, who gets to decide whether we begin geoengineering? Creating a blanket of sun-dimming sulfur in Earth's atmosphere isn't exactly something that all countries will be on board with. Yet a project of this magnitude would impact us all. What if some countries oppose the plan? Do we have the right to knowingly carry out a global experiment even in the face of opposition by some? I don't have the answers to these questions, but I suspect they aren't clear and will only make progress on geoengineering even more difficult. An additional barrier to geoengineering is the public opposition that exists around the topic. Warranted or not, the popularity of geoengineering seems to rank alongside contaminated drinking water and genetically modified foods.

Let's turn now to the not-so-insignificant benefits of geoengineering. Global warming presents an imminent threat to humanity and the greater environment for all of the reasons covered in this book. This includes impacts to coral reefs, forests, biodiversity, the spread of infectious disease, sea level rise, natural disasters, and so on. These impacts are already becoming realized and are projected to worsen with each decade. Even if we halt greenhouse gas emissions today, many impacts will continue through the rest of the century since our emissions to date have already committed us to a certain amount of future warming. Geoengineering on the other hand offers an alternative to this grim scenario. By releasing aerosols into the atmosphere, we could potentially block enough sunlight to compensate for the increased greenhouse effect that we've created, and thus arrest further warming. The reflective properties of sulfate aerosols are already proven, which means geoengineering has a shot at actually succeeding.

An added perk of geoengineering is that its effects would be immediate. In the case of reducing greenhouse gases (still a must!), the proposed actions are very gradual and take decades. This is not the case with geoengineering. As we saw from Chapter 3 with the Mount Pinatubo eruption in 1991, sulfur released into the atmosphere indeed produces global cooling. Of course, we can't wish to exactly mimic a massive eruption, but the same physics would at least be at play with geoengineering.

In one of my final graduate courses at Harvard, an expert on geoengineering came to speak about the topic. The class was full of PhD students specializing in atmospheric science, biology, engineering, public health (me!), and other disciplines. Perspectives on the topic were quite mixed. As we've discussed in this chapter, there are clearly many pros and cons that must be considered. However, one thing the class could all agree on was that climate change is a major threat that must be urgently addressed and that—like it or not—geoengineering represents a viable way to slow warming. For now, however, geoengineering remains widely unpopular and research remains minimally funded. For that reason alone, geoengineering is unlikely to "save us" any time soon.

46

Plants And Animals Will Adapt

This sounds like a reasonable assumption at first glance. After all, species have adapted to all sorts of climatic and geologic changes in the past. Importantly, however, many species have also gone extinct in the past—it wasn't just the dinosaurs! Today, species extinction rates are way up, and *have* been for quite some time thanks to the impacts of human activity. To date, some 800 known species have gone extinct from the planet in the last 400 years, over half of which perished in just the last century—owing mostly to hunting.[26] These are just *known* species. Estimates for *total* extinction are much higher. Today, habitat loss, hunting, and climate change are threating many species, with impacts only projected to worsen. One study out of Brown University estimated that "current extinction rates are 1,000 times higher than natural background rates" and that "future rates are likely to be 10,000 times higher."[27]

Unprecedented extinction rates are leading many ecologists to believe we are currently in the midst of a "sixth mass extinction."[26] Why six? Because there have only been five others in the 600-million-year history of complex life on Earth. Yes, the meteor that darkened the skies and killed the dinosaurs is one of them. Humanity's impact on the planet has reach levels comparable to those of prior catastrophic events, in which 95% of Earth's species ultimately died out. As the globe continues to warm, species extinction will likely accelerate. One team comprised of scientists from 14 institutions and universities around the world estimates that "inevitable" climate change scenarios will lead to a nearly 20% loss of species by 2050, with up to 35% extinction under "maximum" climate change. Impacts would only worsen by 2100.[28] These numbers should be troubling and suggest that species won't just "adapt" to climate change. Some will, but many won't. Not surprisingly, the authors note that "minimizing greenhouse gas emissions" and "returning to near pre-industrial global temperatures as quickly as possible" could prevent much of the projected climate-related extinction from occurring.

Why will so many species fail to adapt as the planet warms? It would seem they can just migrate to areas of favorable temperature, right? In the case of plants, however, this is not the case. While plants can indeed "migrate" over time, as seeds disperse and pop up in new places, they can only migrate so fast. Studies looking at the "velocity of climate change" estimate the pace of temperature "isotherms" (areas of the same average temperature) to be moving poleward at a rate of about a mile per year, give or take.[29] Though slow compared to your average trail runner, this speed is sufficient to outpace many plants, which don't enjoy the luxury of walking. Even agricultural crops are on the move. America's so-called "corn belt," for instance, is heading north as unfavorable conditions have forced farmers in some states to abandon the crop, while farms in southern Canada have nearly doubled their corn production.[30]

In the case of animals, migration is of course much easier. In fact, we're already seeing species beginning to inhabit cooler, more poleward areas, as global temperatures rise. However, the news is not all good for our furry, feathered, and scaly friends. Particularly in the North Pole, animals have nowhere to migrate as temperatures rise and sea ice disappears. The plight of the iconic polar bear is the best-known example of this, having even become the "face" of global warming. As sea ice melts, polar bears are less able to hunt seals—their main food source—causing them to starve at an increasing rate. Thus, in 2008 the U.S. placed the species as "threatened" under the Endangered Species Act. Some estimate that polar bear numbers will decline by two-thirds by 2050.[31] Antarctic species appear less threatened at the moment since warming has not been as dramatic—that is, until recently.

Mountains are fascinating environments that share an interesting characteristic with polar regions, leaving their species similarly vulnerable to global warming. Alexander Von Humboldt in the late 1700s was the first to notice the remarkable similarities between ecosystems at similar elevations around the world. That is, elevation appeared to influence ecosystems in the same way as latitude. As one travels poleward, rainforests give way to temperate forests, which give way to shrubs and grasslands, which ultimately give way to the icy tundra. This interesting transformation, Humboldt found, is the same that one observes when hiking up mountains around the world. The bottoms are most lush, giving way to fewer and smaller plants and animals as one moves higher. The largest of mountains even exhibit frigid pole-like conditions at their summits.

Just as regular species are pushing poleward with rising temperatures, many endemic mountain species are pushing higher up. This may be fine for creatures that inhabit mountain bases. But what about those already near the top. For them, like the polar bear, there's nowhere to go. If you're picturing an inhospitable snowy summit, it's probably hard to image too many animals in jeopardy. But not all summits are snowy. In the tropics, mountaintops are often foggy and cool, and rich in life. Species inhabiting these regions have evolved to such conditions, and are falling under threat as the climate warms and these conditions are lost.

These impacts are perhaps nowhere more real than in the Monteverde Cloud Forest, located some 4,500 feet above sea level in the volcanic mountains of Costa Rica. As its name suggests, this tropical rainforest exists almost entirely among the clouds. Having visited when I was a teenager, I can attest to the invisibility that comes with the foggy air up top. However, as the climate warms, this moisture is diminishing. Warming temperatures are now driving the once-constant clouds up and off the mountains, exposing the underlying forests to higher temperatures and drier conditions. The cloud forest is home to many endemic species, having become one of the most frequented eco-tourist destinations in the world. Ecologists and tourists alike worry that recent climatic shifts may mean "the eventual end of the green mountains of Monteverde," as an article in *Scientific American* put it—it's also why the article labeled Monteverde one of the "11 Natural Wonders to See

231

Before They Are Gone."[32] Again, as temperatures rise, mountain species can only migrate so far upwards, before reaching a dead end at the summit. Just as higher temperatures creep vertically up mountainsides, sea level is similarly encroaching up low-lying islands, threatening both human civilizations and endemic species in these areas as well.

We've talked about some unique ecosystems at the poles and mountains where species are limited in terms of migration. But what about other species? As temperatures rise, they'll be able to migrate just fine, right? Unfortunately not, and the reason has to do with habitat loss and fragmentation, which hampers migratory paths. If an ecosystem in its natural state was to slowly begin warming, we could expect a gradual shift of species toward cooler areas—essentially following the ideal climate zone as it moves. For many species, however, ecosystems aren't pristine and uninterrupted, and therefore present challenges to migration.

Recall from Chapter 43 that that livestock alone now takes up 30% of our planet's land area. This has not been good news for forests and other habitats around the world. Where species may have otherwise migrated, cities, roads, and farms now present major barriers, inhibiting their migration. In many cases, landscapes have been so transformed as to leave native areas as nothing more than isolated pockets of wilderness, presenting a major threat to the "nowhere to go" species who inhabit them. Alarmingly, only 8% of the world's protected areas are expected to "exhibit overlap between current climates and end-of-century climates," according to a 2012 report by the University of California, Berkeley.[33] In other words, the climates of most protected areas will have moved beyond their protective boundaries by 2100. For species that can keep up with the moving climate, this means they will effectively be drawn out of their protected habitats—while species with no place to go will be left to face extinction if they cannot rapidly adapt.

Species loss isn't all about migratory capability. The success of California's already threatened checkerspot butterfly, for instance, is highly dependent on the availability of flower nectar at the time when larval emergence takes place. Over time, the species has conveniently evolved to emerge perfectly in sync with the flowering of its native food plants. The flower gets its pollination and the new butterfly gets its breakfast— symbiosis at its best! However, changes in temperature and rainfall patterns since the 1970s have disrupted the timing of these two events, meaning the hungry butterfly often emerges now without food to consume. During a long-term study of this species around the San Francisco Bay, two of the study populations went extinct due to these causes, one in 1992 and the other in 1998.

In the ocean, global warming is having dramatic impacts as well. In fact, one of the most important types of organisms, on which many other species depend, has come under grave threat as oceans have warmed. Regarded as the "rainforests of the sea," coral reefs encompass less than 0.1% of the ocean floor, yet are home to over a quarter of all marine fish species. Unlike fish, coral can't just up and move. Their calcium carbonate structures take years to mature. Unfortunately, as oceans warm, coral is finding it difficult to cope. According a 2017 United Nations global assessment of coral reefs, "rising atmospheric carbon dioxide caused by human activity is the greatest threat to coral reefs globally, primarily due to ocean warming but also due to ocean acidification."[34]

When coral gets overly stressed, it takes on a white lifeless appearance known as "bleaching." Under best-case future warming scenarios, nearly all of the world's most iconic coral reefs are expected to experience temperature-related mass bleaching events twice per decade, which far outpaces the 15-20 years it takes for these delicate reefs to recover. This is a sobering reality. Scientists say that our coral reefs will not thrive again on Earth until carbon dioxide returns to about 320-350 ppm, a level we're unlikely to see in this century or the next (CO_2 is now about 410 ppm and rising!). Along with Monteverde, The Great Barrier Reef is another one of the "natural wonders to see before they're gone," according to *Scientific American*.[32] The article notes that almost half of the living coral on the reef has already disappeared, suggesting that over time the reef could become "but a skeletal remnant, like those that dot the Caribbean." Along with the beauty and majesty of our reef systems, the social, economic and cultural services from coral reefs add up to about $1 trillion globally in value. Losing reefs will therefore also be expensive.

We've talked about extinction due to the inability of many species to keep pace with global warming and adapt to changing conditions. However, we should also discuss impacts caused by certain species that are adapting too well. No better example comes to mind than the case of bark beetles in the western U.S. and Canada. Because these bugs feed on and reproduce in live trees, they can have devastating impacts on forests.[35] Although bark beetles are native to North America, a balance has historically existed in which both forests and bark beetles have been able to coexist. Unfortunately, rising temperatures in recent decades has begun to tilt the advantage in favor of the bark beetle, thus upsetting this delicate balance.

Typically, cold winter temperatures keep bark beetle populations in check. However, milder winters are now making life easier for these tree-eaters, allowing their populations to flourish. On top of that, reduced precipitation is rendering trees drier and less capable of producing their defensive sap. Consequently, recent decades have meant the loss of literally billions of coniferous trees in forests ranging as far south as Mexico and as far north as Alaska. Several recent outbreaks have ranked as the largest and most severe in recorded history. In the last 20 years, over five million acres of forest have been impacted by bark beetles in Colorado alone.[36] As the climate warms, it's likely that bark beetles will continue to expand their range and cause forest destruction.

Just as bark beetles are taking well to warmer temperatures, the success of other key pests has been documented, in some instances impacting public health. In the case of disease vectors such as ticks and mosquitoes, warmer weather is permitting them to move to higher altitudes and latitudes, have longer breeding seasons, and speed up their viral incubation times. We witnessed this first hand as zika virus reached pandemic proportions in 2016, making its way into the Americas for the first time in reported history. The U.S. and its territories reported over 40,000 cases of the disease during and since that outbreak, with over 7,000 infections occurring in pregnant women. Because of its ability to harm the unborn child, entire populations of women during the outbreak were being advised for the first time to hold off on getting pregnant, in some cases for up to two years. Similarly, the Centers for Disease Control and Prevention (CDC) advised pregnant women not to travel to Miami, which marked the first time Americans had been cautioned against traveling to a part of their own country due to infectious disease.

As climate change brings warmer temperatures and increased precipitation and humidity to some regions, it might seem reasonable to assume that areas where mosquitoes are newly inhabiting will be offset by dry areas they're abandoning. However, recall that major natural disasters such as hurricanes and extreme precipitation are creating more wreckage and flooding than ever before (See Chapter 27). This means more debris and stagnant puddles to form ideal breading grounds for mosquito larva. Also, part of what made the zika outbreak so threatening was that it impacted populations that had never yet experienced the disease.

As global warming creates new favorable habitats for mosquitos, deadly mosquito-borne diseases such as Malaria, West Nile, and Dengue are also beginning to impact new areas. Essentially what we're witnessing is the expansion of tropical diseases beyond the usual tropics, as tropical boundaries shift. Scientists have found that the tropical zones, according to the standard meteorological definition, have expanded about 2 degrees of latitude north and south since 1980, or about 50 miles per decade. This means that about an extra 8.5 million square miles of Earth now experience a tropical climate compared to 40 years ago.

Ticks have similarly been spreading to new areas thanks to milder winters in many regions. Long-term studies in

Sweden, Canada, and the Czech Republic have shown the range of ticks to have doubled in some places.[37] Since ticks cause Lyme disease and other illnesses, this presents a public health concern. Even in the U.S., where ticks are native, the CDC states that "reported cases of tickborne disease have doubled [from 2004 to 2016]," owing mostly to increases in Lyme disease.[38] Ticks are also problematic to native wildlife and pets. In a recent conversation, a local Massachusetts resident framed the tick problem to me in an interesting way. Having spent decades walking his dogs in the woods, and thus calling himself a "pseudo expert on ticks," he explained to me that plucking ticks off his dogs used to be an occasional thing, but the woods are now becoming a problematic place from March until January. "I took at least 10 embedded ticks off my dogs over the last few days alone," he told me.

We cannot talk about climate change and species impacts without talking about invasive species. Invasive species are "outsider" species, usually introduced by humans, which cause harm to native habitats. Many weeds in the U.S. are in fact invasive species that were brought over from Europe. Two characteristics that make invasive creatures invasive are their tolerance to habitat changes and their ability to reproduce quickly. These also happen to make invasive species more resilient to climatic changes relative to their native counterparts. A recent study around San Francisco estimated that under the most severe climate change scenarios, up to 53% of California endemic plants will disappear from the region.[33]

Returning to the top of the chapter, it might comfort us to think plants and animals will just "adapt" as the climate warms. However, evidence suggests otherwise. We're already seeing unprecedented rates of species extinction due to human activity. Climate change is only exacerbating the problem. Importantly, humans are part of this whole thing called "the environment." Beauty and aesthetics aside, we depend on abundant forests, healthy oceans, and rich species diversity to sustain humanity. Should we decide to sit back and watch the collapse of these precious, sensitive, and important ecosystems and species, we are essentially deciding to sit back and watch the collapse of our own. The only difference will be timing, and the fact that we, of all species, could have done something to prevent it.

Solutions

47

Electric Cars Aren't That Green!

When talking about climate change and the different ways we can each minimize our carbon footprints, questions and claims about the true "greenness" of electric vehicles (EVs) and hybrids often come up. First, what do we mean when we say *green*? Since the buzz surrounding EVs and hybrids mostly has to do with climate change and their often-touted "zero emissions" design, plus low fuel costs, the greenness we're talking about relates to greenhouse gas emissions. So, how *green is* the electric car? Let's get to the bottom of it! As it turns out, there isn't really a single answer.

How *green* your car is turns out to depend largely on where you live. Why? Let's digress for a moment to discuss how electricity is produced. Importantly, electricity doesn't grow on trees. It must be generated at a power plant. To produce an electric current, power plants need to create motion. More specifically, they need to produce the rotation of a turbine. This typically involves the production of superheated water, or steam, to drive this rotation. Just as wind turbines capture the energy of air as it passes from high pressure to low pressure areas (as wind), turbines inside power plants capture the energy of hot pressurized water as it travels to lower pressure zones within the power plant system. How power plants differ, therefore, is merely a question of how they harness energy to rotate their turbines.

Power stations can be divided into three general categories based on their energy sources. Fossil fuel power plants are those that rotate their turbines using water heated by the burning of coal, oil, or natural gas. Interestingly, nuclear power plants are fundamentally very similar, except they use heat released by nuclear fission reactions to boil the water. The third category of power stations use renewable energy sources, appropriately named because, unlike fossil fuels and nuclear material, the planet won't run out of fuel. Renewable power stations differ widely in concept, using energy sources that include hydro, solar, wind, geothermal, tidal, and others.

Without getting into the weeds on each renewable resource, suffice it to say that they share a couple of key things in common. As noted, they're renewable. But also, they don't need to create heat to rotate their turbines. The wind already blows, sunlight is already hot, and falling water already flows. Even in the case of geothermal energy, the heat is already there under Earth's surface. All that renewable energy plants need to do is tap into existing energy sources. The second critical commonality is that they don't release greenhouse gases. This is something that is even shared with nuclear power facilities. Because these power stations don't burn fossil fuels, they don't release carbon dioxide, and are therefore "climate friendly." Having laid out the groundwork on electricity generation, let's get back to our question of *green* vehicles!

The reason that the "greenness" of your vehicle depends on where you live is because electricity generation varies by region. In the United States, just over 60% of our electricity is produced from fossil fuels, with about 20% coming from nuclear, and the rest coming from renewables.[1] This means that just under 40% of our electricity in the country can be considered emissions free, or "carbon neutral." Since most states employ a mix of both renewable and non-renewable energy sources, you can safely assume that no matter where you live in the country, your zero-emissions electric vehicle isn't really "zero emissions." Probably the closest you can get to a truly zero-emissions vehicle would be if you drove an electric car in Norway, where nearly all of the country's electricity is produced by hydropower.[2] With that said, a vehicle doesn't have to be zero-emissions to be *greener* than a gas-guzzler. In states that source mostly from clean energy sources, the eco-scale is tipped highly in favor of electric and hybrid vehicles.

In 2012, the California Air Resources board commissioned a full lifecycle assessment to compare the carbon dioxide equivalent emission of conventional gasoline vehicles, battery electric vehicles (BEVs), and hybrids operated in the state.[3] The analysis took into account the manufacturing and disposal of vehicle parts, as well as fuel production, transport, and use. Because the state is powered largely by carbon-free renewables and nuclear, plus lower-carbon natural gas, using only about 5% coal, the analysis found that the carbon dioxide footprint turns out to lean heavily in favor of electrically powered vehicles. In fact, gasoline powered cars were found to produce about twice the emissions of a BEVs and still 50% more than a hybrid. Way to go California! Your green cars are truly green—and by a long shot!

What about other states? In many U.S. states, coal is used as a primary means of electricity generation. Since coal is a big CO_2 emitter, the carbon arithmetic in such states is less favorable to EVs. But by how much? In 2015, The Union of Concerned Scientists carried out a lifecycle analysis of different car types, taking into account the various means of electricity generation across the country.[4] Their results showed that for about two-thirds of the population, driving an average EV produces lower global warming emissions than driving a 50 miles-per-gallon (MPG) gasoline car. For states in the Midwest and Greatlakes region, where coal is more heavily used, EVs were still equivalent to gasoline vehicles that get between 35 to 45 MPG. This means that for gas-guzzlers with lower MPG ratings, the electric vehicles remain the better choice. California, along with states in the Northeast and Pacific Northwest, showed MPG equivalents of about 85 to 135 MPG, thanks to their lower use of carbon-intensive electricity.

Just as the eco-benefit of car types varies across the U.S., it also varies around the world. In France, where most of the country's electricity comes from carbon-free nuclear, or Canada and New Zealand, where electricity comes mostly from hydro and other renewables, EVs can truly be said to be *green*. Similarly, the U.K. and Germany get nearly half of their electricity from carbon-free renewables and nuclear. In these countries, electric and hybrid vehicles, while not quite as *green*, still make sense as climate-friendly options.

The countries where EVs make the least sense to own from a climate change standpoint are China and India. In China, car ownership is increasing sharply as the country undergoes rapid industrialization. However, coal-fired power remains the country's primary source of electricity, thus making electric vehicles less persuasive as a clean vehicle.[5] According to an analysis by Bloomberg New Energy Finance however, EVs in China were still found to be cleaner than gasoline vehicles by 30%.[6]

Wait, what about the batteries of electric vehicles? Word on the street is that they require a LOT of energy to produce and are difficult to recycle. Well, all this is true. But recall that our lifecycle analyses have taken battery manufacturing and disposal into account. When comparing EVs with conventional cars, EVs indeed account for more carbon emissions during the manufacturing phase, thanks largely to the heavy-duty batteries. However, as we take into account the entire lifetime use of the car, the balance begins to tilt in favor of EVs, thanks to their zero fuel consumption. This at least holds when electricity production is not predominantly coal-derived, which is a safe assumption in most places, as we've seen.

While various reports may employ slightly different assumptions or numbers in comparing electric and gasoline vehicles, perhaps arriving at slightly different results, the general message about electric and hybrid vehicles is the same. In regions where electricity is produced by less carbon intensive means, such as by renewables, nuclear, and even natural gas, EVs are by far the way to go. This happens to be a substantial portion of the U.S. In areas dominated by coal, however, the benefits of EVs are reduced, and in some cases may even tilt the other way.

However, even in areas where coal makes up a more dominant fraction of electricity production, it's worth pointing out another factor that we have not yet considered. That is, local air pollution. Whether electric vehicles are truly zero emissions or not, they nonetheless have zero tailpipe emissions (they don't even have tailpipes!). This means substantial benefits from an air quality and human health standpoint. Even in the case of coal-fired electricity, burning fossil fuels at a single power plant a hundred miles from town is better than burning it in our own backyards from thousands of miniature power plants (cars!). That is, even if the overall emission levels are the same, or slightly greater, using electric and hybrid cars at least reduces air pollution around cities and towns, thus sparing residents from a lot of harmful exposure. From this standpoint, even China with its coal-fired electricity may still be better off with EVs. After all, residents in the country have been strangled by thick air pollution for years now as the country has industrialized and ramped up its energy use.

While electric vehicles have a ways to go before we can truly call them "zero emissions," the future looks bright. With each coal plant that is retired, and each solar or wind farm installed, electricity will become increasingly *green*, tilting the emissions benefits increasingly in favor of EVs. Even as gas-fired plants come to dominate more of the electricity mix, the carbon intensity of the electricity grid will continue to lessen, so long as coal plants continue to retire. As you'll see in Chapter 50, this is indeed the case—coal plants have been retiring at a record pace, being replaced instead by *green* energy and natural gas. According to the U.S. Energy Information Administration, even "Chinese coal-fired electricity generation [is] expected to flatten as [its] mix shifts to renewables." This all spells good news for EVs as it relates to being *green*.[5]

An entirely separate issue concerning electric vehicles has to do with the electric charging infrastructure and related costs. As any EV driver will tell you, charging stations are not exactly everywhere. Should EVs continue to grow in popularity, massive infrastructural investments would likely be required to enable adequate charging capabilities. Or, perhaps, battery-swap stations would suffice. In some areas with abundant solar, a company called Envision Solar International is even finding a niche. This company has designed small, mobile solar-powered charging stations that can be easily installed in parking lots and other areas in minutes. Perhaps this is the future of electric charging in sunny states!

Recently, a team led by Harvard physicist David Keith has made advances in cost-effectively turning carbon dioxide into a fuel for automobiles. This represents a carbon-neutral innovation that could potentially power vehicles without requiring any infrastructural changes. Whether EVs become the vehicle of the future, or another innovation takes the lead in the long term, EVs are becoming increasingly adopted globally. While imperfect, EVs typically outperform their gasoline counterparts in terms of emissions, and thus can usually be said to be the *green* vehicle of choice. As low-carbon energy continues to account for a growing share of electricity generation around the world, the carbon footprint of EVs will only continue to shrink—taking these vehicles one step closer to becoming true *green* machines.

48

The Public Is Divided
About Global Warming

It's often believed that the nation is divided on climate change. That is, there is a perception among the American public that roughly an equal number of people either believe or don't believe in climate change—or human-caused climate change at least. The popular notion of a "climate debate" certainly doesn't help. Despite this perception, research has found quite a different story. At the 2017 Citizens' Climate International Conference in D.C., I had the opportunity of hearing a keynote address by Anthony Leiserowitz who directs the Yale Program on Climate Change Communication. Leiserowitz is well known for his research on climate change sentiment around the country.

Based on results from a nationally representative survey of over 2,000 people in 2008, Leiserowitz and his team found that American sentiment on climate change can essentially be divided into six distinct categories, or "Global

Warming's Six Americas," as their study was titled.[7] In the first category you have the so-called *Alarmed*. These are the people who are most engaged with the issue. They are convinced global warming is happening, human-caused, and a serious and urgent threat, and are taking steps in their lives to bring about solutions. In the next category are the *Concerned*, who are also convinced global warming is a serious problem in need of action, but are distinctly less involved in the issue and less likely to be taking personal actions to resolve things. Then we have the *Cautious*. This group also believes global warming is a problem, but is less certain that it's happening and doesn't view it as a personal or urgent threat. In the fourth category are the *Disengaged*, who haven't given the issue much thought, don't know much about it, and are most likely to report an openness to changing their minds about it. Fifth are the *Doubtful* people. This group is split evenly among those who think global warming is happening, those who don't, and those who aren't sure. People in this group often feel global warming is either natural, a problem for future generations only, or something the country has already sufficiently addressed. The sixth and final "America" is the *Dismissive* group, which consists of those we commonly think of as "climate deniers." Like the *Alarmed*, this group is actively engaged in the issue, but oppositely so. Most believe global warming is not happening, is not a threat, and does not warrant a national response.

What's more noteworthy than the mere *division* of America into six categories is the proportion of those who *fall into* each category. Despite popular belief that the country is divided on climate change, Leiserowitz shows that 18% of people are among the *Alarmed*, believing strongly that climate change is happening and that we ought to do something about it, whereas only 7% are among the *Dismissive*. Put another way, there are more than twice as many *Alarmed* people as there are *Dismissive*. If we add up the two categories on both sides of the climate sentiment spectrum, we find that over 50% of people are either *Alarmed* or *Concerned* about climate change, compared to less than 20% who are either *Doubtful* or *Dismissive*. This is a 2.5 times size difference. Even more shockingly, when we compare the proportion of those who would be considered "climate deniers" with those who believe global warming to be a major problem worthy of action, the latter group is over seven times larger! Even those who fall somewhere in the middle are mostly comprised of the *Cautious*, who still believe climate change is a problem. So where is the "divided" public and so-called "climate debate?" What is often thought of as a large population of climate skeptics turns out to be an incredibly small minority.

"Global Warming's Six Americas" suggests something very interesting. While the overwhelming majority of Americans believe that climate change is a threat and must be addressed, an incredibly small group of skeptics have succeeded in dominating the public square on the matter. By being persistently vocal on television, the radio, and other settings, this small group has created the appearance of an evenly weighted debate, despite evidence that suggests this couldn't be further from the truth. While this may sound a bit frustrating to the seven-times-larger group of Americans who are onboard with climate science and want to see action, it also presents an opportunity. If most Americans agree that we have a climate crisis, then there is a real opportunity to mobilize climate policy and address the issue.

In his keynote presentation, Leiserowitz used the National Rifle Association (NRA) as an example to reinforce this takeaway message. Regardless of your views of the NRA or your position on gun ownership in this country, nobody really doubts or questions the power of the NRA to influence gun policy. In fact, their visible influence has become a hot issue of controversy in recent years. Interesting, as powerful as the NRA is, the group consists of only about five million members. Now don't get me wrong, that's a lot of members! However, if our "six Americas" truly reflect the nation, then the numbers are in favor of climate action. That is, if 50% of adults in the country believe climate change to be a serious threat, then we've already got a pool of over 120 million people. Even the NRA membership can't compete with that! Even if we assume just a quarter of those concerned about climate change will rally behind climate action, that's still 30 million people— over six times the NRA membership!

If five million Americans can so profoundly influence gun policy, then 40 million can do the same for climate policy. There is an enormous reservoir of climate action "energy" waiting to be tapped. We just haven't realized it. So what's the difference between the NRA and the climate advocates? Organization! As Leiserowitz points out, it's the NRA's success in organizing that has allowed the group to be so highly effective in advancing its agenda. Meanwhile, many who are concerned about the climate are either silent or still unsure of how to become active on the issue. Meanwhile, those who are engaged are often fragmented between groups and organizations, rather than gathering under a single banner to deliver a unified message to Congress. Thus, federal and international climate policy has languished.

To date, much of the conversation I've encountered with climate advocates at some point turns to the topic of "the climate deniers." If only we could convince them of the truth, then we could begin to address the problem. If we've learned anything from the work of Leiserowitz, however, it's that convincing the deniers is entirely unnecessary. The majority of America already accepts the climate science and is ready to move forward. If we can merely organize this bunch of people, as the NRA and other groups have organized, then we can begin to turn the tide—and potentially even quickly! Climate advocates are beginning to recognize this and, rather than trying to convince the minority, are instead turning their attention on mobilizing the majority.

In writing this book, I'm not expecting to change the minds of the *Dismissive* 7% of Americans. It would be wonderful if I could, but it's unlikely. Rather, I'm hoping to reach the rest of the country. To the *Doubtful*, I'm hoping to clear up some of the confusion that has contributed to their uncertainty and skepticism about climate change. Meanwhile, I' m hoping to provide the insights needed to spark interest and get a climate dialogue going among the *Disengaged*, while instilling a sense of urgency among the *Cautious*. To those who are already onboard and engaged, but wish to learn more about global warming, I hope this book is a useful resource.

Incidentally, the organization hosting the conference where I heard Leiserowitz speak happens to be one of the organizations that are heeding the important message of his

252

research—namely, to organize and mobilize the majority who accept the climate consensus and to deliver a unified message to Congress. Citizens' Climate Lobby (CCL) is a grassroots organization now consisting of around 100,000 members. Their expansion from a single meeting spot in California to over 350 chapters worldwide in just over ten years since their founding is a testament to the climate mobilization that is possible. CCL stresses the importance of avoiding debates with climate skeptics, and instead emphasizes the utility of uniting those who already agree— most of the country—in order to generate the political will for climate policy in Washington. Specifically, they're asking Congress to put a price on carbon (See Chapter 29). Other groups are working on similar goals, as described in the final chapter of this book. The unification and organization that these groups are demonstrating, particularly with respect to a single policy message, represents a critical piece in addressing climate change. It's what is needed!

Although this chapter has focused mostly on Leiserowitz's Six Americas, other polling confirms the absence of a divided public. According to a 2017 Gallup Poll, for instance, nearly 70% of American's said they "believe global warming is caused by humans," with 45% of Americans saying they "worry a great deal about global warming."[8] These numbers agree quite nicely with those who were either *Alarmed, Concerned,* or *Cautious* (70%) about global warming, or just *Alarmed* or *Concerned* (51%), in Leiserowitz's study. Similarly, in a 2017 poll by the widely respected *Associated Press—National Opinion Research Center polling collaborative*, 53% of American's said that climate change is an "extremely or very important" issue.[9] Importantly, this doesn't even count those who think climate change is "pretty" important or "somewhat" important. What about the rest of the globe? In a poll of 40 nations, Pew Research found that majorities in all nations say climate change is a "serious problem," with a median of 54% who believe it is a "very serious problem."[10]

Even in my own research about climate sentiment on social media, I haven't found evidence of a divided public. In preliminary results examining hundreds of so-called "tweets" from Twitter that included the keywords "climate change" or "global warming," the overwhelming majority of tweets call for climate action, express frustration about global warming disbelief, or convey worry about climate-related impacts. Only about 10% side with the notion of a climate hoax or express disbelief about human-caused global warming. This again agrees rather well with Leiserowitz's 7% *Dismissive*. Given the overwhelming evidence about public sentiment on climate change, it's safe to say the notion of a divided public is little more than a mirage—perhaps a relic of the past. Having said that, the next step is to better organize and translate belief and sentiment into action.

49

It's Too Late For The Climate

For some, the prospect of climate change has become overwhelming. The thought of a sizzling hot future with extreme weather, high seas, more droughts, and ecological catastrophe—not to mention governmental inaction—has created an all-too-real feeling of helplessness. When speaking publicly on climate change, I'm often asked whether there's anything we can do at this point about climate change. The answer is a resounding "yes!"

Though I became acquainted with the climate issue at an early age, thanks to my mother, an environmental science teacher, I didn't begin diving into climate science until I was an undergrad at UCLA. It came up in seemingly every science class I took, from tropical climatology, earth science, and geology, to oceanography, atmospheric chemistry, and others. Everywhere I turned, the issue of climate change was pervasive and talked about—not debated, by the way, but rather explained and discussed. Discussion at the time was about "preventing" climate change. The global average

CO$_2$ concentration at that point was still around 385 ppm. In just a decade, I've been shocked to see how rapidly CO$_2$ levels have gone up—now approaching 410 ppm!—with many climate impacts already becoming visible. Consequently, the dialogue has shifted. Scientists today speak less about *preventing* climate change than about preventing the *worst* of it. We cannot prevent climate change because climate change is here and happening. Even if we stop emitting greenhouse gases today, the impacts of our past emissions will continue to influence the climate for decades or more to come. With that being said, all is certainly not lost, and there remain things we can do to ensure a brighter (but not hotter!) future.

While it's true that we've committed ourselves to at least *some* future global warming, there are still a number of climate outlooks moving forward. These outlooks range from mild to severe and depend entirely on how we decide to act today in terms of controlling our greenhouse gas emissions. For instance, as noted earlier, projections for sea level rise by the end of the century range from about 1 to 8 feet. Where we fall in this range depends on how rapidly temperatures continue to rise and glaciers continue to melt. If we keep releasing greenhouse gases into the air at the present rate, we can expect sea levels to approach the upper estimates of that range.

A group of Princeton University researchers exploring the impacts of various global warming scenarios recently showed that even a seemingly small decrease in global warming from 2.0°C to 1.5°C by 2100 "spares the inundation of lands currently home to about 5 million people."[11] In Fahrenheit, this would translate to a decrease from just 3.6 to 2.7 degrees on average. By the end of the century, the study found that New York City can expect three Hurricane Sandy-like floods per decade by the year 2100 if global temperatures rise 1.5°C relative to pre-industrial levels, and four such events if temperatures rise by 2.5°C. The over 150 deaths and $60 billion worth of damage that was caused by Sandy reminds us of the difference one storm can make.

Again, the extent to which we warm the planet depends on *us*. It depends on which greenhouse gas emissions path we choose. Other Princeton researchers have come up with the concept of "climate stabilization wedges." Essentially, these wedges specify the carbon emissions cuts needed to avoid various levels of climate catastrophe. For instance, according to Princeton's Carbon Mitigation Initiative, carbon emissions from fossil fuel burning are projected to double by 2060 (relative to 2010).[12] This business-as-usual scenario would more than triple atmospheric carbon levels, relative to pre-industrial times. This increase would of course warm the atmosphere by some amount, melt glaciers by some amount, raise sea levels by some amount, and cause some added amount of hurricane destruction, drought, etc. However, by taking action and employing various innovative strategies today, using existing technology, we can at least ensure that carbon emissions do not exceeded some designated level and therefore prevent some expected amount of damage. Stabilization wedges represent these specific strategies. The term comes from the fact that carbon emissions cuts would start off small and increase with time, forming a "wedge," or pizza-like, shape.

The Princeton team has come up with 15 separate strategies, or wedges, each of which has the potential to reduce global carbon emissions by at least one billion tons per year over 50 years. They estimate that by 2060 we'll have released about 200 billion more tons of carbon into the atmosphere, compared to 2010. Avoiding this increase entirely and keeping emissions flat for 50 years (an ambitious goal!) would therefore require trimming projected carbon output by about eight billion tons per year by 2060. This corresponds to eight climate stabilization wedges. Examples of just eight of the fifteen stabilization wedges described by the Princeton team include:

Doubling the fuel efficiency of two billion cars from 30 to 60 miles per gallon.

Decreasing the number of car miles traveled by half.

Using best efficiency practices in all residential and commercial buildings.

Increasing wind electricity capacity by 10 times relative to 2010.

Replacing 1,400 coal electric plants with natural gas-powered facilities.

Using 40,000 square kilometers of solar panels (or 4 million windmills) to produce hydrogen for fuel cell cars.

Capturing and storing emissions from 800 coal electric plants.

Eliminating tropical deforestation.

Again, these each correspond to the prevention of one billion tons of carbon from entering the air over 50 years. If combined, these strategies would ensure the eight billion tons of emissions cuts needed to keep carbon emissions flat, moving forward. Though a practical piece of insight, a combination of the entire 15 proposed wedges among other strategies would be a more realistic approach to reaching carbon reductions goals, whether it be a goal of flat emissions or simply less dramatic emissions growth.

In terms of identifying what our carbon emissions reduction goals should be, this task is not so easy and involves politicians, economist, scientists, industry stakeholders, and the public. However, one thing is for sure. If we don't establish a goal, we'll never get anywhere—and certainly not fast enough. Maintaining a business-as-usual track would secure the worst-case-scenario estimates as our reality. Fortunately, as our Princeton friends have shown us, the technologies exist today to rapidly curb carbon emissions and bring about the reductions needed to secure a much safer future for society and for our planet. Achieving this is simply a matter of prioritization.

50

I'm Only One Person; There's Nothing I Can Do

As tempted as I am to recite the words of Mahatma Gandhi or Martin Luther King Jr., suffice it to say that as individuals we *can* make a difference and should strive to *be* that difference. You don't need to lead a movement to be effective as a climate advocate. Whether through lifestyle changes, political engagement, involvement with community groups, or serving as a low-carbon role model in your neighborhood, there are a variety of different ways you can be effective in helping move the world toward a more stable climate. Let's take a look at the numerous ways we can all make a difference and *be* that change we wish to see!

Spread the Message

If you want to talk climate solutions to a crowd in today's world, stepping onto a podium is not a necessity. This is particularly so given the world of social media in which we currently find ourselves. In the old days, you needed to be a professional reporter to document and publish stories, or own a newspaper stand to distribute the day's headlines. Today, with platforms such as YouTube, almost anyone can document a story for the world to see. And with the mere click of a button, platforms such as Facebook and Twitter allow those stories to go viral, whether it be a video, article, or something else.

While social media comes with its drawbacks—Aunt Jane's cat videos or Brian's conspiracy theories!—it also presents an opportunity as a climate advocate. Platforms like Facebook and Twitter are increasingly becoming places where people turn to for their news. That means that nearly each and every person with a laptop or smartphone has the power to be a news reporter. This was not the case a decade ago. Sure, social media will probably always be loaded with all types of unimportant nonsense, but don't let that discourage you from using the platform in constructive ways. Share what's important. Help get the facts on climate change out to the public. There are plenty of good science-based articles from authoritative sources that you can pass on to others.

U.S. Government agencies such as the National Oceanic and Atmospheric Administration, Environmental Protection Agency, U.S. Geological Survey, and National Aeronautics and Space Administration are just a few of the great sources that continuously publish informative videos, charts, and articles that speak to the science and impacts of climate change. Many of these are made simple and easy to understand. Non-profits such as the Sierra Club, 350.org, Climate Reality Project, Citizens' Climate Lobby, and many universities also have educational climate material worth sharing. Take a look at their online content and help move the climate conversation forward by sharing what you find via social media. If you happen to be a teacher, you've got an even better opportunity to educate the public. Many of the organizations just mentioned have developed specific content to help teachers incorporate climate education at all grade levels—and not just for science teachers! Believe it or not, creative ways exist to bring climate change into English, math, and even other disciplines.

When it comes to sharing climate news on social media, you may have a knee-jerk reaction to avoid wanting to be "that person"—the one who talks about global warming, since the topic has sadly become politicized and almost taboo to discuss among unfamiliar company (#awkward!). But now is not the time to be shy. It is not the time for silence. Those who understand the importance of climate change *can* and *should* utilize the new age of social media to spread the message. Those who are already concerned over climate change and trying to engage others about its significance are ahead of the curve. Others will follow suit as the impacts of global warming worsen and as more politicians recognize that Earth isn't partisan. By speaking out, you're reminding friends that climate change is something we *can* and *should* talk about.

Social media sites such as Facebook, Meetup, and others can also be used to connect like-minded neighbors who share a passion for climate action. In fact, many climate groups already exist. Get online and see if you can find any near you. If there aren't any, start one of your own! If you'd rather not meet in person, check out the online-only groups on Facebook. These operate more like chatrooms for the purposes of discussion and sharing news, linking people from all around the world.

Be the Change

In addition to using social media, each one of us plays a role in either demanding more or less energy through the amount that we travel, the products we purchase, and the foods we choose to eat. These personal lifestyle choices and activities have important implications for carbon emissions and climate change which individuals should not overlook. I'm not going to be unrealistic and tell you that by taking a bike instead of a car to work (like I do!) you will spare enough CO_2 emissions to have any noticeable impact on global average temperatures. In truth, there is very little any single person can do to affect the climate through consumption choices and other lifestyle changes.

Fortunately, however, humans don't act and behave in isolation. Friends and family members influence each other in important ways. This is where a ripple effect can come in! Not surprising, those we're close to tend to influence how we vote, what we eat, how we dress, what we think is "cool," and so on. This realization should empower us. It means our individual actions needn't be framed solely in the context of our personal carbon footprints. By riding a bike to work, choosing to eat less meat, or throwing solar panels on our roofs, we're serving as a model for others who may eventually do the same, while reminding them that climate change is a problem.

So, in addition to the few actions just mentioned, what are some important steps we can all take to reduce our greenhouse gas emissions and serve as a model for others?

In 2012, the Union of Concerned Scientists published a publicly available list of the "Top 10 Ways to Reduce Your Carbon Emissions."[13] Let's have a look at their guide.

Switch to a car with better fuel economy. *Upgrading from a 20 mpg car to a 40 mpg car can save you 4,500 gallons of gasoline over the car's life span. At today's gas prices, that's a total savings of more than $18,000.*

Make your house more air tight. *Even in reasonably tight homes, air leaks may account for 15 to 25% of the heat our furnaces generate in winter or that our homes gain in summer. If you pay $1,100 a year to heat and cool your home, you might be wasting as much as $275 annually.*

Buy and USE a programmable thermostat *for a 15% reduction in your heating and cooling emissions and save $180 a year. During the summer, a setting of 78°F is optimal during the hours you are at home, and 85 degrees when you are away during the day.*

Eat less meat, especially beef. *An average family of four that cuts its meat intake in half will avoid roughly three tons of emissions annually.*

Use power strips in your home office and home entertainment center *to curb "phantom loads" and save a surprising amount on your electric bill. Keeping your laser printer turned on when not in use could be costing you as much as $130 annually.*

Upgrade your refrigerator and air conditioner, *especially if they are more than five years old. New ones are twice as efficient or more. For fridges: if they're old an upgrade can pay for itself in as little as three years in energy savings alone.*

Get an electricity monitor *from your local hardware store* or even borrow one from many local libraries to see where the energy hogs are in your home. This can help you save hundreds of dollars annually.

Change those light bulbs. New LED light bulbs can give the same light for 15% the electricity. That adds up to more than $100 in savings for most families each year.

Wash clothes in cold water. They get just as clean with today's detergents. But hot water washes use five times the energy—and create five times the emissions. This could save you nearly $100 a year.

Buy less stuff. Reduce, re-use, and recycle—it's not just about pollution, but the strategy will lower your emissions too and help combat global warming.

At the end of the guide, the authors bothered to tag on an eleventh recommendation to "spread the word," noting that "if all Americans reduced their emissions by 20% we could shutter [shutdown] 200 of the nation's 600 coal plants." This reinforces the importance of the ripple effect we discussed earlier! In addition to the tips just provided, I'll add a few actions of my own, which will not only reduce your carbon footprint, but can also be quite fun lifestyle choices.

Waste less food. Recall that nearly 40% of food ultimately gets wasted in the U.S. Every wasted pound is associated with wasted energy, and unnecessary carbon emissions. Ask for restaurant to-go boxes, eat OR freeze items before they spoil, and don't cook more than you're willing to eat as leftovers.

Hang-dry your clothes. If you live in a sunny place like southern California, hanging your clothes is a no-brainer.

Why waste electricity when you've got solar power right outside? Even without a patio, hang-drying is feasible. Small, collapsible hanging racks are widely available.

Start a compost. In the U.S., food scraps and yard trimmings make up 15% of municipal solid waste.[14] Shipping that waste to a landfill takes energy. By starting a compost, this added fuel use is avoided. If you don't think you have room to compost, think again! When I lived in a small apartment in Boston, a company named Bootstrap Compost did the job for me. For a small fee, they'd come twice per month to pick up my food scraps—leaving behind fresh soil for the garden. Now, living in California, I do my own composting and love it! Watching the transition of food scraps to soil is quite fun and fascinating. And the garden loves it too!

Drink from the tap instead of buying water bottles. In the U.S., towns and cities must comply with federal drinking water standards. Thus, tap water is safe. In fact, bottled water companies use the same stuff anyways. They just charge you for it! By drinking tap, you'll reduce the energy that's wasted shipping water long distances and save money in the process! If you still don't trust your tap, buy a small water filter.

Eat local, yet wise. The less fuel used to ship goods, the lower the carbon emissions. So buy local, perhaps from a farmers market! But distance isn't everything. Ocean shipping is far more energy efficient than land and air transport. So keep this in mind.

Bike when you can! Bike paths exist all over. Find one near you and demote your car to a weekend tool. I currently bike 10 miles to my university and back for work. By the time I return, I've gotten my exercise in, had some outdoor fun, avoided unnecessary carbon emissions, and even saved money on gas!

Regardless of the actions you decide to take to reduce your energy use and emissions, remember to be proud of them, and don't hesitate to inform others about their benefits. No need to be pushy, but no need to hide your good deeds. Actions can't be influential if kept secret.

By making simple changes in your daily lifestyle and inspiring others to do the same, your individual acts can translate into collective action. And *that is* powerful. Individual actions can turn into collective actions which, over time, can grow into a movement. The ability of a movement to meaningfully affect carbon emissions is undeniable, particularly in the U.S. and other developed nations where lifestyles are extremely energy-intensive.

While collective action as consumers is powerful, can we really rely on a movement to get us out of the climate dilemma we've created? Yes, and no! While being energy conscious is important and certainly has a role to play in climate change, it's unrealistic to think that a consumers' movement towards low-energy living will be our golden ticket to a stable climate. Maybe we'll get there someday. But at the moment, developed countries are far too accustomed to energy-intensive lifestyles. We depend on gasoline to run our cars, methane to heat our homes, electricity to power our televisions, computers, and lightbulbs, and the list goes on. In most cases, people aren't even aware of the implications of their energy-intensive activities. Similarly, most have not heard of a carbon footprint.

In the U.S., if a movement did spark and we somehow managed to part with our exuberant energy consumption, the impacts would likely still be offset by the world's two most populated countries, China and India, which are rapidly moving in the opposite direction as they industrialize. In the case of China, the country has been erecting new coal-fired power plants for years to support its growing electricity demand—allowing it to eclipse the U.S. around 2005 as the world's leader in carbon dioxide emissions.[15] A similar coal trend is taking place in India. This is not to say that consumer-side energy reductions in the U.S. or elsewhere would not be good. They would! But waiting around for this to happen is not our best chance at urgently addressing global warming. Fortunately, collective action doesn't end with demand-side economics.

As it relates to energy, supply-side changes offer exciting opportunities that will be critical to solving the climate conundrum. That is, by making changes in the way vehicles operate and electricity is produced, enormous reductions in carbon dioxide can be realized throughout the world. And importantly, such changes can occur on a much more immediate timeframe, since they're often initiated by policy or other top-down changes. To bring about such change, public pressure is a necessity. This is where you and I come in again, and where collective action can be most effectively applied—that is, through political engagement and the ballot box.

Vote for the Climate

Like all industries, the energy sector is heavily influenced by policies and actions at the state and federal level. For instance, government subsidies play a big role in deciding which sectors of the energy economy experience growth and success. When subsidies are allocated for wind and solar projects, we see expansion in these sectors. For decades, the fossil fuel industry has been awarded the lion's share of energy-related government subsidies. Today, while we face a fossil fuel-related climate crisis of global proportions, the industry still receives massive government subsidies. Not surprisingly, the U.S. electricity mix remains dominated by coal and natural gas. How federal subsidies get allocated is something that is decided in Congress. Who gets to occupy each seat in Congress is decided by us, the people of this country. Should the public take a greater interest in energy production and decide to demand actions in Washington, you can bet we'd see results.

The most important climate solutions we can demand from our elected officials have again been conveniently summarized by the Union of Concerned Scientists.[16] They include:

Expand the use of renewable energy and *transform our energy system to one that is cleaner and less dependent on coal and other fossil fuels.*

Increase vehicle fuel efficiency and *support other solutions that reduce U.S. oil use.*

Place limits on the amount of carbon that *polluters are allowed to emit.*

Build a clean energy economy by *investing in efficient energy technologies, industries, and approaches.*

Reduce tropical deforestation and *its associated global warming emissions.*

A specific policy solution that relates to #3 and the idea of limiting carbon pollution is so-called "carbon pricing."

We discussed it in Chapter 29, so no need to rehash the details. Suffice it to say that if we don't want air pollution, then we should make it expensive to pollute. Find out what carbon pricing proposals or other policy solutions are on the table in *your* area or at the federal level relating to energy and climate change. Groups such as the Environmental Defense Fund, Citizens' Climate Lobby, Friends Committee on National Legislation, and others often have information on upcoming policy decisions available on their websites. If climate policy is about to get voted on, politely call your state or federal representatives involved and let them know you support the policy. Phone calls are surprisingly effective. If no such policies are on the table, ask your representatives to be the ones to author a bill. You can even pay a visit to their offices. This is how the political process was designed. Engagement is key!

As of this writing, the 2018 U.S. midterm elections are just around the corner, after which a variety of new members of Congress will arrive in Washington. Let's make sure the right candidates get the job. Regardless of Republican *vs.* Democrat, we need candidates who recognize the threat posed by climate change and intend to do something about it. This is essential not just for 2018, but for every election year moving forward. All too often candidates ignore the topic of global warming. Even in the last presidential election, climate change went virtually unmentioned in the televised debates. This needs to change, and we're the ones to change it. There's no valid reason for political candidates to ignore the topic of climate change in this day and age, and therefore no reason to let them off the hook for it. Simply pick up the phone or pay a visit to the office of your local political figures, candidates, or City

Councils and ask them to talk climate. Inquire about their views and climate action plans. Ask them to pass a resolution requesting Congressional action. Find out if they have an action plan? Do they acknowledge the climate consensus? This is critical to know. Often, such information is available online.

Elected officials are paid by the public and work for the public. Thus, we must ensure that they know, understand, and care about our views and concerns. If they don't, then they don't deserve our support at the ballot box. Sometimes our favorite candidates don't make it through the primary elections. Though frustrating, we mustn't get discouraged and opt out of the final vote for office. If both candidates seem undesirable or too similar, it's more than likely that they at least differ in their positions on climate change—which is still a critical distinction. Thus, if for no other reason than global warming, we must cast a vote. In doing so, we'll have taken the world one step closer to a safe and habitable climate for our generation and those to follow. Since the U.S. is a global leader, climate action here at home will set the stage for other nations to take action as well. Thus, our vote is more important than you might think. Let's make it count!

Get Involved

When it comes to addressing climate change, there's no need to reinvent the wheel. Some very well-established, organized, and effective groups are out there on the frontlines of climate action. They're knocking on the doors of Congress, writing to the local papers, speaking to the public, among other things in order to advance the climate conversation and get climate policies passed across the country. Here are just a few groups to consider. Many others exist, which can be looked up online.

Citizen's Climate Lobby is a non-profit, non-partisan, grassroots advocacy organization focused on national policies to address climate change. CCL is not your rally-in-the streets type, but rather employs a more calm and calculated approach. With the goal of building "political will" for climate solutions, members are taught to follow the political playbook. They reach out to Congress, write to media, network with news stations, etc. CCL is largely focused on getting the federal government to pass a revenue-neutral carbon pricing plan. Their emphasis on shared values rather than partisan divides has enabled them to successfully build relationships with community leaders, elected officials, and others.

Americans for Carbon Dividends is an education and advocacy campaign to build support for a carbon dividends plan recently proposed by the conservative Climate Leadership Council, which was authored by prominent conservative leaders including James Baker and George Shultz. **#PutAPriceOnIt** is also more of a campaign than a group. It's emphasis, as with CCL and ACD, is carbon pricing. A main goal of the campaign is to gain endorsements from college presidents, business leaders, and various organizations to demonstrate to lawmakers widespread support for carbon pricing. Along similar lines, **Students for Carbon Dividends** is a national bipartisan coalition of students and student groups dedicated to propelling a carbon dividends proposal to Congress. **The Alliance for**

Market Solutions represents yet another effort to achieve carbon pricing.

Our Children's Trust is leading a major, youth-driven, climate recovery campaign to secure the legal right to a stable climate and healthy atmosphere. At the heart of its campaign is the *Juliana v. United States* federal court case, dubbed "the trial of the century," being brought by 21 youths from across the country whom, on behalf of themselves and future generations, have sued the U.S. government for violation of their fundamental right to a habitable climate. Through its YouCAN (Youth Climate Action Now) program, OCT supports youth, their families, and others to engage in civic participation with government. They've also created Youth v Gov, for people looking to mobilize in support of their landmark climate case.

Earth Guardians is a youth-led organization dedicated to empowering and supporting other youth to become leaders of tomorrow. Their mission is to "protect the planet for future generations." In 2015, Youth Director Xiuhtezcatl Martinez gained international praise after he addressed climate change in a famous speech before the United Nations at age fifteen. Members of Earth Guardians happen to be among the youth plaintiffs involved in the landmark federal court case on climate change, *Juliana v. United States*. The group therefore works closely with "Our Children's Trust."

350.org is a grassroots organization that was co-founded ten years ago by author Bill McKibben, who wrote one of the early books on global warming. Named after the level of atmospheric CO_2 deemed "safe" for the planet (350 ppm), this organization focusses on campaigns to help build a global climate movement. Some of their efforts include the recent campaigns against the Keystone XL and Dakota Access pipelines in the United States, as well as helping mobilize support around the Paris Climate Accord. They're also active in efforts to pressure universities, foundations, and cities to divest from fossil fuels. The group places an emphasis on climate justice to ensure vulnerable communities don't get left behind. Currently, 350.org includes a network that extends to nearly every country around the world.

Environmental Defense Fund works on a variety of issues, including clean water, clean air, and wildlife preservation, boasting some three million members and 500 scientists, lawyers, and policy advocates. In terms of climate change, NRDC works through the court system to address our dependence on fossil fuels and enable the expansion of clean energy across cities, states, and nations.

Your climate action doesn't have to end with a climate organization or petition. Climate leaders are needed from the grassroots to the treetops. If you're feeling bold and want to join the world of politics, start your own campaign for local office! Here are some groups that are helping pave the way for new incoming political leaders.

RunForSomething.net is an organization dedicated to helping recruit and support young diverse candidates to run for down-ballot races in order to "build a bench for the future." The group lowers the barriers to entry for these candidates by offering financial support, organization building, and access to the training needed for success.

314action.org is a non-profit organization that is dedicated to getting more scientists elected to public office. The group boasts a rapidly growing 400,000 members, with over 3,000 scientists who have already signed up for political training. As of this 2018 publication, more than 200 scientists are running for federal or state offices, which is the largest number in modern U.S. history. Go scientists!

Stay Hopeful

Understanding the seriousness of climate change can be a heavy weight to bear. At times, the outlook seems grim and the solutions daunting. However, staying hopeful is critical if we're to succeed in doing what is needed to stabilize the climate. Fortunately, there are plenty of reasons for such hope and numerous examples of progress. Let's take these final paragraphs to acknowledge some of the most promising developments in the world of climate change solutions. After all, what better way to close out our final chapter than on an *up* note?

Thanks in large part to the work of the Citizens' Climate Lobby (CCL), we have some good news in the realm of politics. That is, for the first time in history Republican and Democratic members of the U.S. House of Representatives have been brought together on a massive scale in support of climate action. This has taken the form of the House Climate Solutions Caucus, which was founded in February of 2016 by two south-Florida representatives, Republican Carlos Curbelo and Democrat Ted Deutch. Despite its recent inception, the Caucus already boasts 84 members (42

Republicans and 42 Democrats) who are actively focusing on policy options to address the "impacts, causes, and challenges" of climate change. The bipartisan design of the Caucus means that members must join in pairs, so that there is even weight between the two parties. This Caucus represents a remarkable political achievement that *The New York Times* called "a promising step toward sanity" and "one of the first efforts to break the partisan impasse." In the period since Donald Trump gained the presidency, membership to the Caucus has grown by four-fold! This suggest a potential turning tide for carbon emissions.

Along the lines of bipartisan progress, February of 2017 marked the publication of an important document called the Conservative Case for Carbon Dividends.[17] This plan calls for putting a price on carbon dioxide pollution. However, this is not what makes the plan significant. Importantly, it was authored by prominent Republicans such as James Baker, former Secretary of State under President George H.W. Bush, and George Shultz, former Secretary of State under President Ronald Reagan. While many Democrats have accepted the notion of global warming and the need for carbon pricing for quite some time, this publication represents a first and very important step towards the same recognition and goal by prominent conservatives. "Mounting evidence of climate change is growing too strong to ignore," the authors note. Such bipartisan acceptance of a climate crisis and the need for action is crucial to addressing climate change. This publication suggests that we're getting there.

Other evidence of a turning tide has recently been seen at the ballot box. In terms of carbon pricing, such a policy made it onto the ballot in 2016 as Initiative 732 in

Washington State. The state's neighbor to the north, British Columbia, implemented a similar program in 2008, which served as the foundation for the state initiative. Initiative 732 would have made Washington the first U.S. state with a carbon tax. Though defeated due to some kinks to be worked out, the initiative nonetheless represented a first key step towards a low carbon future. Moving forward in time, that same carbon proposal is now back on the table—or at least a new iteration of it is back. In November of this year (2018), voters in Washington will decide again whether to enact what would become our country's first state-level carbon tax! This time it's in the form of Initiative 1631.[18] In Utah, this year also saw the first ever bipartisan carbon fee introduced in a state legislature.

Revenue-neutral carbon pricing is foundational to our ability to reduce greenhouse gas emissions and stabilize the climate on a scale and timeframe that is meaningful. There aren't a whole lot of strategies, if any, that can accomplish the same thing, particularly on a global scale. Thus, these political developments on carbon pricing are wonderful news. And that's not even where it ends. On the other side of the country, Massachusetts just had a carbon pricing bill pass the state Senate. The bill not only passed with bipartisan support, but with unanimous support. This vote marked the first passage of a revenue-neutral carbon pricing plan by a U.S. legislative body."[19] The bill must still pass the House, but it nonetheless suggests momentum in the right direction. Working tirelessly behind the scenes to pass carbon pricing are the many volunteer-based organizations we discussed previously. And excitement about the recent developments are palpable. As one state-level carbon pricing coordinator from CCL put it, "There are moments when, after years and years of relentless efforts, movements see a sudden wave of transformation. For the movement to put a price on carbon, 2018 could be that moment."[20]

Let's turn to energy. Coal, the dirtiest and least climate friendly of the fossil fuels, has recently been on its way out in the U.S. According to the U.S. Energy Information Administration, coal accounted for over 80% of retired electric power plants in 2015.[21] According to reporting by the Sierra Club, 10 of the 12 worst environmental justice offending coal plants happen to be on the list of those either retired or proposed for retirement.[22] In general, nearly all of the U.S. powerplants that retired in the last decade were powered by fossil fuels. In fact, just this year Colorado's biggest utility, Xcel Energy, filed a plan to retire two of its coal units, and instead replace them with the biggest package of clean energy ever proposed in the U.S. for an individual coal retirement—consisting of wind, solar, and gas sources. This is all great news for the climate!

On the topic of *green* energy, electricity generation from renewable sources has skyrocketed over the last fifteen years. Production of solar power in the U.S., for instance, quadrupled in the last five years alone.[23] The story for wind power is similar, having increased by about five times in the last 10 years. For the first time in 2017, monthly electricity generation from wind and solar exceeded 10% of total electricity production in the U.S.[24] Even in California, where the energy mix was already pretty *green*, renewables (not even counting large hydro) have come to account for an added 20% of electricity production in just the last decade—effectively tripling! This is not only good given our standard uses of electricity, but also brings electric vehicles

(EVs) one step closer to realizing their true *green* potential.

Let's talk more on EVs. In 2017 the International Energy Agency reported that new EV registrations hit an all-time record, with over one million sales worldwide.[25] Norway was most impressive, with electric cars having accounted for nearly 40% of their new car sales! As for the future, EV sales are likely to keep booming. The global electric car stock exceeded one million vehicles in 2015, only to cross three million two years later. Meanwhile, research, development, and mass production are leading to rapid battery cost declines that are helping to narrow the cost competitiveness gap between EVs and standard gasoline cars. While there is still a long way to go before EVs account for a dominant share of total on-road vehicles, things are certainly headed upward.

Internationally, the world cringed when President Trump dealt what looked to be a major blow to the climate with his decision to withdraw the country from the Paris Climate Accord. However, this announcement was met with immediate defiance from U.S. governors and mayors from coast to coast who pledged to uphold their commitments under the Accord in order to carry the nation onward in reducing global warming.[26] From my own state, California Governor Jerry Brown flew to Paris to say "We're here, we're in and we're not going away."[27] This mobilization on the part of U.S. leaders is reassuring. Also noteworthy, in the final stages of this book's completion, U.S. Environmental Protection Agency (EPA) director Scott Pruitt announced his resignation. Pruitt was a Trump appointee with a proven disdain for environmental policy and climate science. It was ironic that he should have headed the EPA to begin with. It's unclear as to who Pruitt will be replace by. However, nobody with a concern about climate change is sad to see him go.

As we try and make headway on climate solutions, no force is like that of the public. For this reason, whether it be climate policy or behavioral change, public sentiment on climate change is crucial. That is, people have to *care*. Fortunately, they are—and increasingly so, which is perhaps the most positive news of all! Especially in the U.S., where climate change sentiment tends to fall along party lines, the public is gradually awakening to the reality and impacts of global warming. According to a recent Gallup Poll, American concern over climate change is higher today that at any point in the last three decades.[8] This is particularly important because the U.S. has such a critical role to play in reducing greenhouse gas emissions and leading the world forward. Not only are we the second largest greenhouse gas emitter, but we're also a global leader economically and often set the bar when it comes to environmental protection. Were the U.S. to finally make climate policy a priority, there is little doubt we'd see a ripple effect around the world. Other nations would more rapidly jump aboard, and climate mitigation measures would accelerate. Fortunately, nations haven't waited around as the U.S. has languished on climate action. Nonetheless, a growth in American climate concern would be globally significant. The fact that the younger generation tends to be most concerned about climate change is yet another piece of positive news that should make us sleep better at night. Assuming they carry their views into their older years, the world may be getting passed to a safer set of hands.

Myself among this younger generation, I intend to remain

vigilant about human activities and their impacts to our health and the well-being of our planet. This book is one manifestation of that. Hopefully, in some way, this work will have contributed to a turning tide on climate change and inspired climate actions that would have not otherwise occurred. Regardless of background or political affiliation, most people want what's best for our environment and for this planet. Even those who disregard global warming are not doing so because they don't care about the planet. Rather, they don't think the planet is in jeopardy. The dynamic between climate activists and climate skeptics is therefore not one of "good *vs.* evil," but one of "knowing *vs.* not knowing." If you've made it this far in this book, you are among the *know*. It's now important to share with friends, family, and coworkers all that you've come to understand both here and elsewhere about climate change, and thus contribute to the *know*. The faster we can all come to understand and discuss climate change, the faster we can replace misconception with fact, and lay the groundwork for action. Let's get to work!

Notes

Climate Science 101

1. *U.S. Environmental Protection Agency*, Inventory of U.S. Greenhouse Gas Emissions and Sinks: 1990-2016, 2018.
2. *Intergovernmental Panel on Climate Change Fifth Assessment Report*, Working Group III, Mitigation of Climate Change. Summary for Policymakers, 2014.
3. James Hansen, *Storms of My Grandchildren: The Truth About the Coming Climate Catastrophe and Our Last Chance to Save Humanity*, 2009.
4. *U.S. Environmental Protection Agency*, Atmospheric Concentrations of Greenhouse Gases, 2016.
5. Stephen Montzka, Non-CO2 Greenhouse Gases and Climate Change. *Nature*, 2011.
6. *National Snow and Ice Data Center*, Methane and Frozen Ground, 2018.

Natural Change

1. Yuzhen Yan and Colleagues, 2.7-Million-Year-Old Ice from Allan Hills Blue Ice Areas, East Antarctica

Reveals Climate Snapshots Since Early Pleistocene, *Goldschmidt Conference*, 2017.

2. Dieter Lüthi and Colleagues, High-Resolution Carbon Dioxide Concentration Record 650,000–800,000 Years Before Present, *Nature*, 2008.

3. Terry Gerlach, Volcanic Versus Anthropogenic Carbon Dioxide, *EOS Transactions American Geophysical Union*, 2011.

Climate Conspiracy

1. John Cook and Colleagues, Quantifying the Consensus on Anthropogenic Global Warming in the Scientific Literature, *Environmental Research Letters*, 2013.

2. *The White House*, Restoring the Quality of Our Environment, Report of the Environmental Pollution Panel President's Science Advisory Committee, 1965.

3. *U.S. Atomic Energy Commission*, the Environment and Ecological Forum 1970-1971, 1972.

4. *Secretariat of the World Meteorological Organization*, Proceedings of the World Climate Conference, 1979.

5. Hearing on Ozone Depletion and the Greenhouse Effect, 1986.

6. Leo Hickman, Police Close Investigation into Hacked Climate Science Emails, *The Guardian*, 2012.

7. Brian Winter, Scientist: Leaked Climate E-Mails a Distraction, *USA Today*, 2009.

8. *National Research Council of the National Academy of Sciences*, Himalayan Glaciers: Climate Change, Water Resources, and Water Security, 2012.

9. Stefan Rahmstorf and Colleagues. Comparing Climate Projections to Observations Up to 2011, *Environmental Research Letters*, 2012.
10. Seth B. Darling and Douglas L. Sisterson, *How to Change Minds About Our Changing Climate*, 2014.

Doubt

1. *American Chemical Society*, Chemists and Chemistry that Transformed Our Lives, 2017.
2. Susan E. Strahan and Anne R. Douglas, Decline in Antarctic Ozone Depletion and Lower Stratospheric Chlorine Determined from Aura Microwave Limb Sounder Observations. *Geophysical Research Letters*, 2018.
3. *U.S. Environmental Protection Agency*, Progress Report on the EPA Acid Rain Program, 1999.
4. *U.S. Global Change Research Program*, Climate Science Special Report: Fourth National Climate Assessment, 2017.
5. George Marshall, *Don't Even Think About It: Why Our Brains are Wired to Ignore Climate Change*, 2014.
6. Neela Banerjee and Colleagues, Exxon: the Road Not Taken, *Inside Climate News*, 2015.
7. Geoffrey Supran and Naomi Oreskes, Assessing ExxonMobil's Climate Change Communications (1977–2014), *Environmental Research Letters*, 2017.
8. Christine Dell'amore, "Snowball Earth" Confirmed: Ice Covered Equator, *National Geographic*, 2010.
9. Luann Dahlman, Climate Change: Global Temperature, *National Oceanic and Atmospheric Administration*, 2017.

10. *National Oceanic and Atmospheric Administration*, 2017 was 3rd Warmest Year on Record for the Globe, 2017.
11. Pieter Tans and Kirk Thoning, NOAA ESRL Global Monitoring Division, *National Oceanic and Atmospheric Administration*, 2018.
12. Bob Taylor, Together We Can Continue to Raise the Voice of Science and Ensure a Safe, Stable Climate, *Los Angeles Times*, 2018.
13. William Nordhaus, *the Climate Casino: Risk, Uncertainty, and Economics for a Warming World*, 2015.
14. Andrew E. Dessler and Colleagues, Water-Vapor Climate Feedback Inferred from Climate Fluctuations, 2003-2008. *Geophysical Research Letters*, 2008.
15. *U.S. Environmental Protection Agency*, Greenhouse Gas Emissions from a Typical Passenger Vehicle, 2018.
16. *The World Bank*, CO_2 Emissions (Metric Tons Per Capita), 2018.
17. Tom Gillespie, Great Barrier Reef Dead at 25 Million, *The New York Post*, 2016.
18. *Australian Research Council Centre of Excellence*, Coral Reef Studies: Annual Report 2017.
19. *Australian Research Council Centre of Excellence*, 2016 Global Coral Bleaching, Annual Report 2016.
20. Lauren Shoemaker, Stable and Radiocarbon Isotopes of Carbon Dioxide, *National Oceanic and Atmospheric Administration*, 2010.
21. *U.S. Environmental Protection Agency*, Coal-Fired Power Plant Emissions, 2006.

22. Doug Dockery and Colleagues, An Association Between Air Pollution and Mortality in Six U.S. Cities, *The New England Journal of Medicine,* 1993.

23. Fabio Caiazzo, Air Pollution and Early Deaths in the United States, Part I: Quantifying the Impact of Major Sectors in 2005. *Atmospheric Environment,* 2013.

24. *World Health Organization*, Burden of Disease from Ambient Air Pollution for 2012, 2014.

25. Press Release, IARC: Outdoor Air Pollution a Leading Environmental Cause of Cancer Deaths, *International Agency for Research on Cancer,* 2013.

26. *WHO International Agency for Research on Cancer*, Air Pollution and Cancer, 2013.

27. Paul Epstein and Colleagues, Full Cost Accounting for the Life Cycle of Coal, *Ecological Economics Reviews,* 2011.

28. *NOAA National Centers for Environmental Information*, Billion-Dollar Weather and Climate Disasters: Overview, 2018.

29. *Intergovernmental Panel on Climate Change*, Climate Change 2014: Synthesis Report, 2014.

30. Michael E. Mann and Kerry A. Emanuel, Atlantic Hurricane Trends Linked to Climate Change, *EOS Transactions, American Geophysical Union*, 2006.

31. James B. Elsner, Evidence in Support of the Climate Change—Atlantic Hurricane Hypothesis, *Geophysical Research Letters*, 2006.

32. *California Department of Forestry and Fire Protection*, Top 20 Most Destructive California Wildfires, 2018.

33. *California Department of Forestry and Fire Protection*, Top 20 Largest California Wildfires, 2018.

34. *Oregon Live*, Oregon's Largest Wildfires, 2018.

35. *National Oceanic and Atmospheric Administration*, Climate at a Glance, 2018.
36. Leroy Westerling and Colleagues, Warming and Earlier Spring Increase Western U.S. Forest Wildfire Activity, *Science*, 2006.
37. Ruben Vives and Colleagues, Southern California's Fire Devastation is 'The New Normal,' Gov. Brown Says, *La Times*, 2017.
38. Yongqiang Liu and Colleagues, Future U.S. Wildfire Potential Trends Projected Using a Dynamically Downscaled Climate Change Scenario, *Forest Ecology and Management*, 2013.
39. John Hopewell, nearly 50 inches in 24 Hours — Hawaii May Have Broken the National Rainfall Record, *The Washington Post*, 2018.
40. *NOAA National Centers for Environmental Information*, Contiguous U.S. had its Warmest May on Record, 2018.

Jobs and the Economy

1. Richard J. Lazarus, *The Making of Environmental Law*, 2004.
2. Paul Epstein and Colleagues, Full Cost Accounting for the Life Cycle of Coal, *Ecological Economics Reviews*, 2011.
3. *Citizens Climate Lobby*, Legislative Proposal: Carbon Fee and Dividend, 2018.
4. Scott Nystrom and Colleagues. the Economic, Climate, Fiscal, Power, and Demographic Impact of a National Fee-and-Dividend Carbon Tax, *Regional Economic Models, Inc.*, 2014.

5. James A. Baker and Colleagues, the Conservative Case for Carbon Dividends, *Climate Leadership Council*, 2017.

6. Christopher Ingraham, The Entire Coal Industry Employs Fewer People Than Arby's, *The Washington Post*, 2017.

7. Rory Mcilmoil and Evan Hansen, Coal and Renewables in Central Appalachia: the Impact of Coal on the West Virginia State Budget, *West Virginia Center on Budget and Policy*, 2010.

8. *U.S. Energy Information Administration*, Annual Energy Outlook 2018, 2018.

9. *U.S. Energy Information Administration*, Even as Renewables Increase, Fossil Fuels Continue to Dominate U.S. Energy Mix, 2017.

10. *U.S. Energy Information Administration*, Coal Power Generation Declines in United Kingdom as Natural Gas, Renewables Grow, 2018.

11. *U.S. Department of Energy*, U.S. Energy and Employment Report, 2017.

12. *Agency International Renewable Energy*, Renewable Energy and Jobs: Annual Review 2017, 2017.

13. *NOAA National Centers for Environmental Information*, Billion-Dollar Weather and Climate Disasters: Overview, 2018.

14. David J. C. Mackay, *Sustainable Energy—Without the Hot Air*, 2009.

15. *Environmental Working Group*, The United States Farm Subsidy Information, 2016.

16. Ilaria Espa and Sonia E. Rolland, Initiative: Subsidies, Clean Energy, and Climate Change. *International Centre for Trade and Sustainable Development (ICTSD) and World Economic Forum*, 2015.

17. *Management Information Services, Inc.,* 60 Years of Energy Incentives: Analysis of Federal Expenditures for Energy Development, 2011.
18. *Environmental Law Institute,* Estimating U.S. Government Subsidies to Energy Sources: 2002-2008, 2009.

Conflicting Evidence

1. Kate Ramsayer, Antarctic Sea Ice Reaches New Record Maximum, *National Aeronautics and Space Administration,* 2014.
2. Maria-Jose Viñas, NASA Study Shows Global Sea Ice Diminishing, Despite Antarctic Gains, *National Aeronautics and Space Administration,* 2015.
3. *National Oceanic and Atmospheric Administration,* Sea Ice and Snow Cover Extent, 2018.
4. Maria-Jose Viñas, Sea Ice Extent Sinks to Record Lows at Both Poles, *National Oceanic and Atmospheric Administration,* 2017.
5. *National Oceanic and Atmospheric Administration,* Global Temperature: Global Land-Ocean Temperature Index, 2018.
6. Daniel Grossman, Why Our Intuition About Sea-Level Rise is Wrong, *Nautilus,* 2016.
7. *National Aeronautics and Space Administration,* Glacial Rebound: The Not So Solid Earth, 2015.
8. Shfaqat Abbas Khan and Colleagues, Geodetic Measurements Reveal Similarities Between Post-Last Glacial Maximum and Present-Day Mass Loss from the Greenland Ice Sheet, *Science Advances,* 2016.
9. *National Snow and Ice Data Center,* Quick Facts on Ice Sheets, 2018.

10. *Polar Portal: Monitoring Ice and Climate in the Arctic,* End of the SMB Season Summary 2017, 2017.
11. Andrew Evans, Is Iceland Really Green and Greenland Really Icy?, *National Geographic,* 2016.
12. Robert Ferguson, *The Vikings: A History,* 2009.
13. Michael Mann and Colleagues, Global Signatures and Dynamical Origins of the Little Ice Age and Medieval Climate Anomaly, *Science,* 2009.
14. *U.S. Global Change Research Program,* Climate Science Special Report: Fourth National Climate Assessment, 2017.
15. David Archer, *The Long Thaw,* 2009.
16. José M. Vaquero, Historical Sunspot Observations: A Review, *Advances in Space Research,* 2007.
17. David C. Lund and Colleagues, Gulf Stream Density Structure and Transport During the Past Millennium, *Nature,* 2006.
18. Jason Samenow, Baked Alaska: 49th State is Having an Insanely Warm December, *The Washington Post,* 2017.
19. Amy Goodman, "Freakishly Warm" Arctic Weather Has Scientists Reconsidering Worst-Case Scenarios on Climate Change, *Democracy Now!,* 2018.
20. Gerald A. Meehl, Relative Increase of Record High Maximum Temperatures Compared to Record Low Minimum Temperatures in the U. S., *Geophysical Research Letters,* 2009.

The Flip Side

1. Annie Sneed, Ask the Experts: Does Rising CO2 Benefit Plants?, *Scientific American,* 2018.
2. *U.S. Environmental Protection Agency,* What Climate Change Means for California, 2016.

3. Mandy Freund, Multi-Century Cool- and Warm-Season Rainfall Reconstructions for Australia's Major Climatic Regions, *Climate of the Past*, 2017.
4. Rachel Kleinman, No More Drought: It's a 'Permanent Dry', *The Age*, 2007.
5. Karl Hille, NASA Study: Rising Carbon Dioxide Levels Will Help and Hurt Crops, *NASA Goddard Institute for Space Studies*, 2016.
6. Charles T. Garten, Litterfall N-15 Abundance Indicates Declining Soil Nitrogen Availability in a Free-Air CO_2 Enrichment Experiment, *Ecology*, 2011.
7. *U.S. Global Change Research Program*, Climate Change Impacts in the United States: The Third National Climate Assessment, 2014.
8. Dana Gunders, Wasted: How America is Losing Up to 40 Percent of its Food from Farm to Fork to Landfill, *Natural Resources Defense Council*, 2012.
9. Sonja J. Vermeulen, Climate Change and Food Systems, *Annual Review of Environment and Resources*, 2012.
10. Henning Steinfeld, Livestock's Long Shadow: Environmental Issues and Options, *Food and Agriculture Organization of the United Nations*, 2006.
11. Åsa Stenmarck, Estimates of European Food Waste Levels, *Food Use for Social Innovation by Optimising Waste Prevention Strategies (FUSIONS)*, 2016.
12. Alisha Coleman-Jensen, Household Food Security in the United States in 2010, *U.S. Department of Agriculture*, 2011.
13. Luann Dahlman, Climate Change: Global Temperature, *National Oceanic and Atmospheric Administration*, 2017.

14. *Intergovernmental Panel on Climate Change Fifth Assessment Report,* Working Group I, Projections, Commitments and Irreversibility, 2013.
15. Jonathan Belles, All-Time February Heat in the Southern Plains, *The Weather Channel,* 2017.
16. *National Oceanic and Atmospheric Administration,* Weather Fatalities, 2017.
17. Rebecca Lindsey, 2017 Arctic Report Card: Extreme Fall Warmth Drove Near-Record Annual Temperatures, *National Oceanic and Atmospheric Administration,* 2017.
18. Michon Scott, February 2018 Heatwave Across the Far North, *National Oceanic and Atmospheric Administration,* 2018.
19. Jason Samenow, Baked Alaska: 49th State is Having an Insanely Warm December, *The Washington Post,* 2017.
20. *National Aeronautics and Space Administration,* Long-Term Warming Trend Continued in 2017: NASA, NOAA, 2018.
21. Bill Mckibben, *Eaarth: Making a Life on a Tough New Planet,* 2011.
22. Maria-José Viñas, Arctic Wintertime Sea Ice Extent is Among Lowest on Record, *National Aeronautics and Space Administration,* 2018.
23. *Polar Portal: Monitoring Ice and Climate in the Arctic,* End of the SMB Season Summary 2017, 2017.
24. *U.S. Global Change Research Program,* Ch. 16: Northeast. Climate Change Impacts in the United States: Third National Climate Assessment, 2014.
25. Tom Di Liberto, Record Warmth in February 2018, *National Oceanic and Atmospheric Administration,* 2018.

26. Fred Pearce, Global Extinction Rates: Why Do Estimates Vary So Wildly?, *Yale School of Forestry & Environmental Studies*, 2015.
27. Jurriaan Michiel De Vos, Estimating The Normal Background Rate of Species Extinction, *Conservation Biology*, 2015.
28. Chris D. Thomas, Extinction Risk from Climate Change, *Nature*, 2004.
29. Scott R. Loarie, the Velocity of Climate Change, *Nature*, 2009.
30. Alan Bjerga, Corn Belt Shifting North With Climate Change, *The Washington Post*, 2012.
31. Stephen Leahy, Polar Bears Really are Starving Because of Global Warming, Study Shows, *National Geographic*, 2018.
32. David Biello, 11 Natural Wonders to See Before They are Gone, *Scientific American*, 2015.
33. Todd E. Dawson and Colleagues, Potential Impacts of Climate Change on Biodiversity and Ecosystem Services in the San Francisco Bay Area, *University of California, Berkeley*, 2012.
34. Scott F. Heron and Colleagues, Impacts of Climate Change on World Heritage Coral Reefs: a First Global Scientific Assessment, *UNESCO World Heritage Centre*, 2017.
35. *United States Department of Agriculture,* Bark Beetles in California Conifers: Are Your Trees Susceptible?, 2015.
36. *Colorado State Forest Service*, 2017 Report on the Health of Colorado's Forests: Meeting the Challenge of Dead and At-Risk Trees, 2017.
37. Filipe Dantas-Torres, Climate Change, Biodiversity, Ticks and Tick-Borne Diseases: the Butterfly Effect. *International Journal of Parasites and Wildlife*, 2015.

38. Ronald Rosenberg and Colleagues, Vital Signs: Trends in Reported Vectorborne Disease Cases— United States and Territories, 2004-2016, *U.S. Centers for Disease Control and Prevention*, 2018.

Solutions

1. *U.S. Energy Information Administration*, June 2018 Monthly Energy Review, 2018.
2. *International Hydropower Association*, Norway, 2017.
3. Kimberly Aguirre and Colleagues, Lifecycle Analysis Comparison of a Battery Electric Vehicle and a Conventional Gasoline Vehicle, 2012.
4. Rachael Nealer and Colleagues, Cleaner Cars from Cradle to Grave: How Electric Cars Beat Gasoline Cars on Lifetime Global Warming Emissions, *Union of Concerned Scientists*, 2015.
5. *U.S. Energy Information Administration*, Chinese Coal-Fired Electricity Generation Expected to Flatten as Mix Shifts to Renewables, 2017.
6. Jim Efstathiou Jr. and Dave Merrill, How Green Is Your Electric Car? *Bloomberg*, 2018.
7. Anthony Leiserowitz and Colleagues, Global Warmings Six Americas 2009: An Audience Segmentation Analysis, *Yale Project on Climate Communication*, 2009.
8. Lydia Saad, Global Warming Concern at Three-Decade High in U.S., *Gallup, Inc.*, 2017.
9. *The Associated Press-NORC Center Public Affairs Research*, Views on President Trump's Job Performance, 2017.

10. Bruce Stokes and Colleagues, Global Concern About Climate Change, Broad Support for Limiting Emissions, *Pew Research Center,* 2015.

11. Michael Oppenheimer and Colleagues, Extreme Sea Level Implications of 1.5 C, 2.0 C, and 2.5 C Temperature Stabilization Targets in the 21st and 22nd Centuries, *Environmental Research Letters,* 2018.

12. *Princeton University Carbon Mitigation Initiative,* Stabilization Wedges Introduction, 2018.

13. *Union of Concerned Scientists,* Top Ten Ways to Reduce Your Carbon Emissions (and Save Money at the Same Time), 2012.

14. *U.S. Environmental Protection Agency,* Municipal Solid Waste, 2016.

15. *PBL Netherlands Environmental Assessment Agency,* Trends in Global CO_2 Emissions: 2013 Report, 2013.

16. *Union of Concerned Scientists,* Global Warming Solutions: Reduce Emissions, 2018.

17. James A. Baker and Colleagues, The Conservative Case for Carbon Dividends, Climate Leadership Council, 2017.

18. Yoram Bauman and Joe Ryan, Will Washington Voters Warm to a New Carbon Tax Initiative?, *The Seattle Times,* 2018.

19. Bruce Mohl, Putting a Price on Carbon Gains Momentum in Mass, *Commonwealth,* 2018.

20. Jamie Demarco, Carbon Pricing Bill Passes Massachusetts Senate, *Citizens' Climate Lobby News,* 2018.

21. *U.S. Energy Information Administration,* Coal Made Up More Than 80% of Retired Electricity Generating Capacity in 2015, 2016.

22. *Sierra Club*, Moving Beyond Coal, by The Numbers, 2017.

23. *U.S. Energy Information Administration*, Electric Power Monthly, 2018.

24. *U.S. Energy Information Administration*, Wind and Solar in March Accounted for 10% of U.S. Electricity Generation for First Time, 2017.

25. *International Energy Agency*, Global EV Outlook 2018, 2018.

26. Dakin Andone and Nicole Chavez, U.S. Mayors, Governors Vow to Stick With Paris Accord, *CNN*, 2017.

27. Brown Reaffirms U.S. Commitment to Paris Agreement With Michael Bloomberg at COP23: "We're Here, We're in and We're Not Going Away", *State of California: Office of Governor*, 2017.

Acknowledgements

I would first and foremost like to thank my family and friends who supported me and shared in my enthusiasm as I embarked on this project. Thank you to my loving girlfriend Athina for bearing with my countless late nights as I worked hard to complete this book. Your patience, support, and excitement throughout the writing process and in life has meant the world. Thank you to my amazing mother Teri for the energy and insight you bring to all my projects. This book was no exception. I'm grateful to my grandfather Tom for your unwavering support and advice throughout this project, and all else in life. And to my brother Jalal; thank you for your invaluable friendship and support, and for your writing insights and critiques early in my life, which helped craft me into the writer I am today. To the four of you just mentioned, I also cannot thank you enough for taking time out of your busy lives to read and provide feedback on this book. Thank you to my sister and photographer Shadia, who made sure we had just the right photo for this publication.

My dearest thanks to my former professor, friend, and mentor Arthur Winer for reviewing the early draft of this manuscript and offering substantive improvements that shaped this book for the better. Your guidance and insight has been so important in my life, and your feedback on this book was no less valuable. Thank you to Mark Tabbert for your enthusiasm and support, and for your help in reviewing and improving select chapters of this text. Your climate advocacy work and the work of Citizens' Climate Lobby is nothing short of an inspiration. Thank you Bob Taylor; you offered a thoughtful and thorough review of the manuscript, which is so very much appreciated. Finally, I am extremely grateful to Craig and Nancy Smith from Dockside Sailing Press for sharing in my vision for this book and helping me to bring it to fruition. You have gone above and beyond in supporting my work and have truly been a pleasure to work with.

A Note about the Font:

Cambria is a transitional serif typeface commissioned by Microsoft Corporation and distributed with its *Windows* and *Office* programs. It was designed in 2004 by Jelle Bosma. Cambria Math, the font used in this book, is a later variant designed for mathematical and scientific texts.

Index

3

A

B

California Governor and climate change activist, *132, 279*

C

R

S

T

Tyndall, John
Scientist did experiments on Green House effect in 1800s, 23, *84*

U

V

W

X

Y

Z

21551566R00178

Made in the USA
Columbia, SC
22 July 2018